i

Designed by Brad age 8

THE ESSENTIAL CREATIVITY OF AWARENESS

By

Veronica Lavender

First published 28/10/2008

Second publication 3/4/2014

ISBN: 1497326567

ISBN-13: 978-1497326569

Other books by Author

Parallel Lives

Embrace the Power Within

The Empowered Affirmations Balancing Technique

Jack the Ripper & the Ghost of Mary Jane Kelly

ACKNOWLEDGEMENTS

I would like to say thank you to my children, Debbie, David and Karen who have been a great inspiration to me, and for their continued love and support.

I would like to say thank you and I'm so proud of you, to my grandson Brad who designed my book cover when he was only 8 years old.

I would also like to thank my dear friends, Kathy, Lin, Karl, and Andy for hours of discussions, their support and encouragement.

Thank you to my family and friends, who have played an important part in my life and to Sue Spears for her guidance, and the art of kinesiology.

I would like to say thank you to Caroline Robinson for the psychic drawings.

I dedicate this book to all who have touched my life in so many ways. Thank you

INTRODUCTION

We all at sometime or other, wonder what life is all about, with us travelling many pathways searching for what we feel is missing within our lives. We often look to others to fulfil some of our many needs, not realising that only we can actually achieve what we need or want. Our lives are a great adventure with us enjoying the different aspects, and challenges, as we experience life, not always getting it right because we don't really know what's expected of us.

Over the years, and whilst experiencing the different aspects of my life's purpose and learning's, I'd hypothetically travelled the universe and back again, in search of what I felt was missing from within my life. I'd experienced the different situations and circumstances within my life, in order to gain the understanding of why certain things had happened to me, and was part of my life's purpose. At times, I felt like I was being punished for a crime I hadn't committed, and whilst searching for the truth, I gained great in-sight into the real reasons why they'd happened, and also experiencing a journey of self-discovery which spanned over many lifetimes.

I meditated on a regular basis to realign myself with the universal and earth's energies, and that of my own inner self, gaining insight, and an understanding into the mysteries behind the hidden messages, and the well kept secrets. My journey has taken me over 30 years, and it was the journey of my soul's quest, discovering my true self, which allowed me to become my truth once more. I have accomplished this by the understanding of the illusions behind my actions and interactions with others, and also the understanding of mirror images, and coincidences that are given to us everyday.

I have also experienced the different holistic techniques and their unique benefits, and how they can help us to self-heal, and reconnect us to our truth. My journey of the inner-self as allowed me to understand how our Mental, Physical and Spiritual Being, integrates and works with our unique energy system of the charka's and our aura. We also need to understand the significance of disabilities, disease, illness, symptoms and conditions, and how our bodies speak to us in order to promote well being.

When we understand our lessons and life's purpose, we can evolve to the higher vibrations of our higher consciousness. This promotes unity of nature, mankind and our spiritual awareness which reawakens us to our dreams and limitless potential of long ago. We can then access the infinite knowledge and wisdom, and the universal laws that allow us to understand how they influence all that we do, with codes of ethics, and conduct. This reconnection to the life force energy of creation is important to continued growth, and existence within the structure of our world.

Our past lifetimes play a big part, in which we really are, and the understanding and importance of the hidden messages and secrets to the real us, will set us free. We all need to embrace our true characters, which helps us to understand our unique gifts, skills, and abilities, which are the characteristics of the real us, and our potential to succeed in every aspect of our lives.

Our spirit guides and angels are significant to our evolutionary journey, but most of all they will help us to reconnection to our true self, for they all hold an important part of us that aid us in achieving our true-destiny and dreams. There is no time scale to our inner journey, the important thing is, that when we are ready we will take the souls journey and achieve the quest of reconnecting with our true selves and truth, once more. This is the person that we know ourselves to truly be, but with us displaying our negative traits, or being influenced by the outward influences that distract us from our true-self and what we want to achieve or accomplish. We all at times focus on others, not realising we're important too. Often telling ourselves we're okay, when in fact we're not.

When we unleash our gifts, skills, and abilities, we will realise they're the natural unique attributes of the inner us, and our knowing thoughts. By understanding our strong instinctive feelings, and acting upon them, would lead us away from danger, pain or self-inflicted procrastination. Our emotions are a positive attribute, and in no way dismiss their true importance, because without them, we would not be able to realise the imbalances or the disharmony within, and they give us a well-balanced view of our lives.

We all have these natural skills, and abilities within, and if understood they become our own mystical gifts of the unknown. These gifts can be used to the highest good of all, and they give us access to our Esoteric knowledge of all past lifetimes, and the Akasha records of our personal records of all our achievements and accomplishments. Once accessed, will provide us with all that we need, spiritually, mentally, personally or even emotionally, allowing us to become our limitless potential of all lifetimes and helps us to achieve our dreams.

The journey of the spiritual awakening is upon us all, and with The Golden Age of Aquarius helps us all on our individual journey of our souls quest, reconnecting us to the power of the creator that within us all, and to accomplish things beyond our wildest dreams. Now that is our power of intention, and truth!

PREFACE

I was born in Wolverhampton in 1953, and I have lived throughout the Midlands area for most of my life. I have three children and grandchildren, and I consider myself to be very lucky with what I have achieved. I experienced times of anguish and traumatic situations that made me really struggle with certain aspects of my life. At times I was so unhappy that I actually wanted out of this lifetime, but after completing the first part of my inner journey, I realised that everything that happened to me, was all part of my life's purpose and the divine plan, making me appreciate all that I've now become, and have within my life.

I find myself writing this book with the intention of helping those, who too, want to overcome their difficult times, but more importantly to understand the reasons why they happened. We have all got different lessons to understand and overcome that will set us free to enjoy the life that was intended, once we'd overcome our life's purpose.

I first learned the art of mediation when I was 28 years of age, it made such a big difference to my life, and it opened many doorways into the unknown, it was a very exciting time. I experienced the many different spiritual gifts, all of which had just one main purpose, to reconnect me to my higher conscious self. This journey allowed me the opportunities to realise, and reach my full potential, but a journey that's ongoing in order for me to reconnect with my limitless potential of all lifetimes.

Over the years I have organised self-awareness classes, mediation groups, and different workshops on the numerous aspects of spirituality, and the holistic techniques, and their unique benefits. I teach the importance of connecting with our unique gifts, skills and abilities, and everything that we need is within us, and provided by the universe and our creator. It's about reinventing and rediscovering our authentic self, allowing each individual to transform their lives consciously.

I live my life to full, and embrace the challenges within my life in order to overcome them in truth, love, and light. With the reconnection of the different aspects of my true self, life really is just an extension of which I've always been, but I now live my life without my negative traits and emotions. When I understood my life's learning's, I became my true-self by being accepting of all things within my life. This process allows us to achieve our dreams effortlessly, and I am happier, more contented.

When I was able to be more accepting of all that happened within my life, allowed me to be at one with myself totally. I no long give myself an hard time because I felt I'd let me down or failed in someway, so I no longer procrastinate because I now accepting of everything and everyone, has part of my life's journey. With the realignment of my true-self, and the positive attributes of my inner being, I feel I'm on the right pathway for the first time in a long time. The understanding of my past lifetimes has played a big part in the journey of my life's purpose, and with me recognising and reconnecting with my true-self.

I am healthier after overcoming the different ailments and discomforts; I now go with the flow of life, accepting what life brings and living life to the full. I now understand the mirror images, synchronicities and coincidences of life's intervention, which keeps me on the pathway to enlightenment, a natural process of self-awareness, attracting all that I need to live abundantly within my chosen life style. But more importantly, it really is a life worth living, because it's a place where dreams really do come true, and miracles are be performed.

CONTENTS

CHAPTER 1

THE ILLUSIONS OF LIFE

What are our illusions in life all about? In past lifetimes we had issues and conflicts that affected our mind, body and soul. On our deaths the negative vibrations of which was carried forwards, because within any lifetime the demise of our death, will be a direct result of an emotional or suppressed anxiety that we'd stored within. Our life's purpose is about alleviating those imbalances so we can gain the greater understanding of the life that was intended for us, a long ago. Instead, we've created lives with pain and grief, all because we've allowed us to stray from the source of our truth, and higher conscious self that would have sustained a healthy life.

We create the illusions within our lives hoping that we'll feel better about us and our circumstances. How do we know what is really expected of us, and how can we fully appreciate the lessons that life demands from us, in order for us to recognise our truth, and evolve successfully? All of us will have doubts about some aspect or other within our lives, whether in our childhoods, adolescent or even our adulthood years. How we perceive the different events that happened to us within our lives, will leave us wondering what they were all about, and too why some of the experiences had created issues, disharmony or imbalances within us. Everything that's happened throughout our lives was meant to happen, and the way we perceived those events, are the understandings to those lessons, and to how we overcome them, all part of our life's purpose.

We have all come into this lifetime to overcome mistakes that we made in past lifetimes or within this life, they are our miss-understandings of situations that happened to us, and left us struggling with certain aspects of our lives. These are

1

lessons that we've pre-agreed to learn from, and will allow us the understanding of their true meaning's. This enables us to be fully in our lives, so we can reconnect to our truth and true-selves once more. If we're not connected to our true selves, it's because we had disconnected from our higher consciousness long ago, and this lifetime is about reinstating that connection. We need the experiences of life, in order to understand the difference between our perception of the positive and negative events that's happened. This allows us to fully understand, and overcome our life's purpose and lessons, enabling us to achieve the understanding of those events in order to reconnect us to the secrets of our existence?

We have come into this life to understand what's really behind the mask of which we truly are, and because we're not connected to our truth. We all have unrest within our souls, that's created the insecurities or emotional imbalances, because of the illusions that we've allowed to influence all that we do. These illusions can be about our pride or ego, and at times out of desperation, frustration or even emotional anguish, in fact any negative emotion that's created from the imbalances within our lives, and over the years has taken its toll. It's also about us not accepting all that happens to us, because with acceptance we would not cause us pain or grief. We came into this lifetime to do exactly what we're in fact doing, all being part of life's purpose, and the divine plan in order to learn from.

It's human nature for us to say that we're ok, when in fact we're not. Sometimes we don't recognise the imbalance or the disharmony within, not realising what's going on, until we begin to feel unwell or even feel blocked in what we're trying to achieve. We all lead busy lives that we don't recognise how the negative imbalances has already started to affect us. We create imbalances even as a small child, adolescents and throughout our adult years, depending what happens to us. These imbalances are created out of hurt or anger, and of feeling unloved or uncared for, as well as emotional trauma. If the imbalances are left undetected, they would eventually cause us concern, and our health would be compromised. As we live our lives, we take on more and more negative disharmony, storing the negativity deep within, without us even realising that we had.

The negative attributes of our emotional, physical or mental disharmonies, are caused by the different situations or circumstances, within our lives, and how we'd perceived them wrongly. We have to deal with our problems, but only when the time becomes right for us to do so. Until then, they cause us to lose touch with reality, and to what's really going on within our everyday lives, to the point where we are not even sure of what is actually real anymore. This leaves us not recognising our truth, which creates even more unrest within us as we continue to struggle.

Out of our unhappiness, we will do things that will create temporary happiness, this gives us a false sense of security; something which is short lived, creating a comfort zone, all because we didn't recognise what's wrong, and what we really wanted within our lives. We often end up kidding or even denying ourselves, and the difference between what we want, and what we need in life, is an illusion.

We often find ourselves doing things within our lives just to make us feel better about us, because of the temporary imbalances that we have created for ourselves. We travel many pathways trying to find what we feel is missing, and sometimes walk around in a blind fog, not sure of where we are going, let alone as to the reasons why? The illusions of life give us daily challenges; they also create times of concerns as we over stretch ourselves. We get very disillusioned, needing a rest from the mental pressures or stress and tension, that we've created for ourselves, and with us endlessly trying to work it all out. So what is expected of us? Why do certain things happen to us that create the unrest within, and at times repeat the same mistakes, over and over again?

To be able to understand these illusions, would give us the answers to our learning's. When we don't learn them, the outcome to whatever we've set out to achieve, never quite works out the way we intended or hoped for? We have all thought at sometime or other that we're hard done too, the efforts we put in, is not reflected in the rewards that we receive. It's amazing how our lives depend on certain things, we tell ourselves that we have to have this, that or the other, self-justifying the reasons as to why we need them. Often telling ourselves they would make our lives easier or make us feel better, maybe we're feeling down or depressed, and fearful that our efforts will end in failure.

At times we crave excitement within our lives or even thinking that we just need a change from what we are doing, because life can get monotonous. But whatever we do, we always find ourselves eventually back to square one, where we become despondent or disillusioned. We create the illusions in life; out of the negativity of what we think would make us happy, instead of what actually makes us happy, because our perception of life can be very limiting of the way we perceive the different situations, us, and others, with us often procrastinating because things are not as we intended them to be. We often get confused, needing to justify our actions, all because we don't believe in us anymore, maybe losing faith, confidence, focus, and direction. We must allow our lives to flow, without the restraints and restrictions, otherwise we begin to feel the pressures because we're trying to get things right.

As we experience life, and evolve to the higher vibrations, our perception of the different situations or circumstances altars. We are influenced by how we feel, and what we think is going on within our daily lives. Everything that happens to us will play a big part in how we perceive what we are doing, also to the reasons why we are doing them. We are all driven through life by what we think we want, and not necessarily by what we need but to focus on what we have

4

already achieved or accomplished, will allow us to feel fulfilled and content within our everyday lives.

To experience the different aspects of our lives, and in understanding our actions, and the interactions of others, will make a big difference to how we then view our lives. We get too involved with issues, paying too much attention to the things that we have no control over or to what hasn't happened yet, focusing on our negative attributes instead of the positive ones. We need to know how to deal with our emotions or feelings, because the more we go through life the more knocks we have, which will continue to cause us problems. We seem to go through life having tried our best, only to find that it was still not good enough.

What is it that we're really supposed to be doing? We tell ourselves that we have to be kind, caring, considerate, and be a good citizen, with us working hard, the list is endless. The problem is that we push ourselves too hard, and then we become too tired, feeling exhausted or even physically ill. All because we didn't recognise the illusions of our actions, and the real reasons behind them being influenced by our hidden agenda of our life's purpose. This is what confuses us by not recognising what is real. To be able to recognise the real reasons behind our actions, we must view life with a positive mindset, because we then stand more chance of solving our problems. When we have a negative mindset we become blinkered, and then we do things for all the wrong reasons.

We all at sometime or other overload our minds, by trying to work our issues out, from this perspective we then change our minds so many times because we become confused, and we're not able to see the wood, for the trees. We become so involved with the different situations or circumstances within our lives that it clouds the issues, which then influences our actions, and the lessons that we needed to learn, just keep eluding us. When we find the solution to our problems or difficulties, the solutions are sometimes just common sense, and at times find ourselves dismissing the obvious, because it seems too simple to be the solution to our problem.

When we think the world is against us or when we feel alone or deserted, we lose touch with reality. We become vulnerable and desperate, seeing things from just our own point of view, but by communicating with others, a problem shared is a problem halved. When we seek advice or ask for support, our problems don't seem quite so bad. Even to sleep on a problem, will enable us to view it differently in the morning, which gives our higher conscious self the opportunity to influence right action during our sleep state.

What is the lesson of the different circumstances or situations, within our lives, and why do they affects us on every level of our being? It's about being in touch with the bigger picture of life, and to be able to understand the events that's happened, and to how they have affected us. It's about being truthful with us, and to attune to the mind, body and soul. When we understand the real reasons behind our emotions, and feelings, we need to be honest with how we're really feeling, maybe we feel neglected, unloved or are we not being considerate to our needs? Some of us have come into this life with issues, problems or even that of illness or disease already in place, and need to be overcome. Our learning's start as soon as we are born, and whatever we're exposed to affect us, our higher self will try to influence us into solving our problems consciously. But first we must be able to listen to the voice within us or that of our knowing thoughts in order to solve our problems.

As we travel through life, we experience many adventures, some we absolutely adore, and others we have mixed feelings about. As we learn and grow, so does our perception, altering our state of conscious awareness. If we were to give the same adventure but to two different people, they would both perceive it differently. We must take into account their different backgrounds, belief's, and personalities, but more importantly to consider their emotional problems or state of minds at that particular time. A lot will depend on the individual to their perception of the event, and to what they perceived to be true. Sometimes we need things to be true in order to justify how we feel, but it's a thin line between what we perceive to be true and what we needed to be true? Firstly it depends if we need it to be true in order to function or to survive within our everyday lives, because of our emotional state. When we're able to experience any event in an un-detached way, we will perceive it truthfully.

As we continue to learn, we go through life attaching ourselves to beliefs, concepts, people, material wealth, aliments, illness or disease. Also our emotional, physical or mental conditions are sometimes fed by the negative aspects within our lives. Just say we have attached to these situations or conditions for security giving us an emotional crutch, why would we do that? To make ourselves feel better because of the disharmony within, we then need to understand why we have the disharmony in the first place. When we can successfully do this, we then do things for the right reasons.

Our life's learning's are about us recognising our truth, helping us learn these valuable lessons, instead of being influenced by the illusions of our learning's. We are often given mirror images which help us to recognise what's true, and what we need within our lives. With all lessons learned our perceptual state of awareness alters with every understanding, and creates a shift in our consciousness.

This lifetime is about reconnecting with all that we pre-agreed too, before we came into this lifetime, in order for us to reach our limitless potential of all lives. The truth of that agreement was erased from our memories at birth, but deep within our sub conscious is the secrets, and messages behind that agreement, and to what influences our actions, and the interactions with others. The power of our knowing thoughts will lead us to the truth of that agreement, and saves us from pain or grief.

How we see ourselves is not as others see us, so again which is the real us? A lot depends on both people to how they view themselves or others; we only get a true picture of ourselves, once we have been totally honest with us. Until then, the real us is influenced by our negative traits, it's like we are two different people. There is one part of us who is All Knowing which the higher self is, and the other part of us who is searching for the truth, which is our lower self. The pathways we have chosen are the right pathways for us, and everything that we do is what we are supposed to do, along with every decision we make or action that we take, are they the right choices for us, but hopefully making them without the negative tendencies of our learning's. When we're having a good day, and we are happy and vibrant, everything is so easy to achieve and that's our higher conscious self, and when we're struggling with our lives then that's our lower conscious self influencing all that we do with our pre-programmed lesson.

There is a reason why we have illness, ailments or disease, and if we can understand why we have these problems in the first place, we then begin to recognise how our defence mechanism works, and how our minds, and physical bodies are working out of harmony. We are all pre-programmed with the various problems but not necessarily realising that we are, so we create the illusions out of ignorance, and a lack of understanding of our life's purpose.

When we have disharmony within, the bodies functions are not as they should be, so they start breaking down. Our bodies demand attention, hoping that we will stop doing the things that cause us stress and tension. Our bodies display these discomforts hoping we'll take notice, and then make changes within our lives. If we do this, we can miraculously change the way our bodies feel, and by changing our mindset we can alleviate the aliments, illness, and the conditions, which eventually creates disease. We can then achieve Well Being within our physical bodies once more, realigning us to

8

our higher conscious self, where we can then alter our perception of the different events, within our lives.

The illusions are what confuse us, our perception to the different situations, people or circumstances are very limiting, and we need to experience life to the full, in order to understand and overcome all lessons. We then gain the wisdom, which is needed before we can truly understand what our lives are all about, and only then can we truly understand what's expected from us. Only we can know our own personal level of truth because it's unique to just us, but it can be all very misleading, especially if we don't really know how to be totally honest with us. It's about us recognising, and being aware of our true feelings, of any given situation or circumstance, it's so easy to mislead the self by doing things that we don't really want to do but find us doing them anyway.

Once we have understood the significance of why we do certain things within our lives, we can then understand what the truth to our actions is. When we're not our truth it could be our emotional state or even that of our pride or ego that helps us to create the illusions or problems, but once we understand that our actions can represent elements of our truth, we are more aware of the illusions.

When realising our errors, we no longer hold onto the negatives, achieving the realisation of purposeful action and intention, creating successful outcomes for all. When we have understood how our minds create the illusions that perfectly match our insecurities, we then learn our lessons and how to be honest with us once more. A bad experience only stays that way if we hadn't learned from it, and by being open to the illusions; we can actually laugh at our mistakes. When we find it easy to laugh at ourselves, we will know that we are getting it right, because we will no longer take life to seriously or personally, and we no longer hold onto the unhappiness of our negative experiences.

When I was growing up, I thought that my Grandmother did not love me; she picked on me all the time, turning mirrors to the wall, and telling me I was vain. She always picked fault with what I did, saying I was always missing when there was chores to be done. She picked on me for absolutely anything, making me feel isolated, and indifferent to what was going on, and also with my siblings. I found myself always on the outside of life, looking in. I had one sister and three brothers at that time, with another sister later on in my childhood; my grandmother had her favourites, making it very obvious that I was not included. My brothers and sister did not seem to notice my grandmother's feelings towards me, but my parents did, but even with their intervention, things did not improve.

My grandmother was very strict; I could not understand what I had done to warrant her behaviour towards me, so throughout my childhood I tried everything to get my grandmother to like me, even to the point where I would do anything for her just to gain her attention or please her. But the more I did, the worse it got, I was persistent, and I never gave up trying. This was my mindset for years, I still visited my grandmother after I was married, taking my own children to see her, but still the situation continued. I felt like I was searching for this love that now had created a void within me, and nothing seemed to fill it. When my grandmother died, I had this overwhelming feeling that she had loved me, but I was still left wondering why it had been the way it had, with me perceiving that she didn't like me.

My perception of that particular time had its negative traits, which I thought I could do nothing about, but it also had a positive effect on me, because I hadn't realised I was determined never to let my own children feel as I had. I made sure that they would never experience the lack of love that I'd felt from my grandmother, showing them the importance of expressing love, and of being able to receive and to show their love. But for me personally I was still searching for that love, it had created a pain within my heart. Years later, on addressing issues within, I realised that my grandmother had done what

10

she had, because it was part of my learning's, and it was a lesson I'd pre-agreed to learn.

My grandmother treated me the way she had because it made me search for a love that I thought I was lacking or missing, eventually finding it, but not in another person but within myself. That was one of my life's lessons, only I could give myself the love that I craved, and to give it to myself unconditionally. I realised that no other person stood a chance of really making me truly happy, because until I'd found the love within myself, I hadn't been in a position to love myself properly or anyone else for that matter. So my perception of that particular time was not as I'd originally thought, because it was tainted with the negativity of my learning's, and the insecurities within me had made me perceive the lack of love the way I had, to understand the importance of self-love.

When my marriage ended in divorce, I felt like my heart had been broken into a million pieces, but because of my perception of the events throughout my married life, my heart had carried the negative imbalances of all those learning's. Once I'd understood the lessons, I was able to heal my heart of all the negativity which I'd stored within from my unhappiness, emotions of hurt, betrayal, despondency and rejection. I am now free to allow my heart its full potential to love, but not just to love myself but to be able to truly love others, whole-heartedly and unconditionally.

The illusions of life are because we don't do things within our lives truthfully. We do what we have to do because we're meant too, so by being accepting of what we do, allow us not to take the negativity onboard, and would eventually set us free. This gives us the understanding of our actions which gives us the knowledge to know what we can change within our lives, gaining the wisdom to recognise our truth, and be accepting of what we can't change. This was to be one of my most important lessons that I'd come to learn from this lifetime; it was a lesson that was part of my life's purpose, and allowed me to see the truth. It taught me to be fully accepting of all the different aspects within my life, and that of others.

The day that I walked down the garden path with my grandmother's sister years after she'd died, was a day I will never forget, for she told me that my grandmother had been very proud of me, and too what I'd achieved, expressing how much alike she thought we'd been. We had both achieved our own businesses, buying and selling of merchandise, and working hard over the years. She told me that my grandmother had kept all of my letters that I'd sent to her over the years, telling her of our intentions, and achievements. She expressed how much the letters had meant to her, because after my grandmother's death they had found them all tied up with ribbon, and stored in her bedside table.

I have always aspired to my grandmother, she was my mentor, and I'd admired her strengths, she had been content, enjoying the simple pleasures of life. My grandmother had lived by herself for over forty years; she died at the grand age, of eighty-six. Without the lessons that I'd learnt from her, and too how I perceived them, I would not be the person I am today, and in a position to be writing this book. I really did not know what was expected of me as a small child, but to live the life as it was intended, will eventually bring us all to the truth about our lives, and what's required from us. This process will enable us all to keep moving forwards, eager to learn the next lesson, even when it appears that we don't always get it right. We all have to live our lives to the full, and experience all aspects of our lives consciously, until the time becomes right, for us to know more.

When I recognised my truth, it was with the realisation that what we need from life is the opportunities to express ourselves in all that we do, loving ourselves, and to be IN LOVE with life. I now feel totally liberated, joyful, and I am set free from my negativity, ailments and fears. I am really glad that she'd been my grandmother, and played her part in my life's learning's, as are all the people that are within our lives.

She may have had other lessons for my brothers and sisters, but only they will really know their perception of their own lessons, and to what they were all about.

I often wonder if they too had understood the significance of the events that had happened within their own lives. I have enjoyed my journey of self discovery because without asking the questions as to why these things happened, I would never have understood the bigger picture of my life. I personally would not have travelled my spiritual quest, a journey that's spanned over 30 years, and a journey where I have hypothetically travelled the universe and back again, in search of my own personal truth. I know my grandmother is around me even now, observing all that I do. So to you Grandmother, I love you.

Over the period of our life, we will realise that everyone, and everything within our lives is helpings us to learn our lessons or to understand our purpose, and everything is how it was intended. It's not that we do not love ourselves, it's just that the negative traits of our learning's will have a negative effect, and at times makes us fall out of love with us, as well as others. As time goes by, our understandings alter which allows us to recognise that we're not really unhappy, we just thought we were. The truth is we do love ourselves, and always have; our unhappiness is just for the duration of our learning, because we actually lose sight of our love for ourselves all because of the insecurities within. When this happens we make others a projection of what we think is lacking within our lives, and when they fail to match our expectations, we see it as a downfall of our beliefs or standards, and our unhappiness overrides any reasonable solution to our problems.

We must be careful that these illusions within our lives don't make us fall out of love with ourselves, because we then blame others for our short falls, and for what's wrong! The mirror image is that at the same time, the people within our lives are doing a similar thing, not always about the same

13

negative trait but maybe an opposite emotion. But an emotion that makes them too search for the things that they think are lacking within their lives, as they also project their fears, negative beliefs, and hidden agendas on to us.

Everything that happens is for a reason, and it's for us all too successfully understand, and learn from, regardless of what we think are our mistakes are! We must be truly accepting of who we really are and of others too, and what happens to us is what's meant to happen. Our insecurities will create the illusions in our lives, a product of self-disbelief, mistrust or fears, all a projection of our negative mindset. Our actions and interactions with others are important to our learning's, as we all help each other do what we're meant to do. With all situations within our lives, our true-self will be inspiring us on, and our higher conscious-self will be guiding us through each process. Our intuitiveness will let us know what's right or wrong, which encourages us in our continued learning's. Our lower conscious-self, feeds our negative mindsets, which creates the illusions, and the problems that affect our everyday lives, in order to learn from.

Our thoughts are the conflicting issues; should I do this or that, changing our minds because we get confused about what to do. We have to take such a lot into consideration, and by the time we make a decision we've already created the imbalance with us which blocks or self sabotages our efforts. So whatever we do, it will be with an underlining negative emotion, with us feeling guilty. We then have to justify our actions, whatever the situation or circumstance is we then end up by not enjoying the experience to its full potential.

CHAPTER 2

OUR TRUTH

What is our TRUTH? Our truth is behind our thoughts, actions, and deeds. Our truth is the engine within our physical body that drives us through life, and like a car we break down from time to time; having a complete overall by the time our life is over. Our truth is not something we can buy or loan, our truth is what we'd pre-agreed and achieved, before we came into this lifetime, and is the truth about the purpose to our life. So where do we store this truth? Life would be so much simpler if we were connected to our truth right from the start, but if we didn't have to search for it or earn it honestly, it would not be worth having because we wouldn't have recognised it has our truth. Our life's purpose is to understand the truth of all things within our past, present, and future.

Our truth is our driving force; it's the fuel, the power behind the engine of our physical body. It is our own personal power, and our ability to do or act, its vigour, and energy are our source, and reconnects us with our inner self. Our truth is like the lessons we have when learning to drive a car, once we've passed our test, the learning's really start as we're now driving the car on our own. Our driving force is our truth, and we have to fine tune the understanding of our responsibility, and our ability to focus on the road ahead, as we journey along on our life's path. We need to react to the little surprises that may come our way, and to be vigilant, cautious, and keeping a watchful eye on the direction we're going, as we continue to travel through life. We need to be able to look at the bigger picture, and seeing the events that might unfold, but then being prepared for them. With all life's lessons they prepare us for all eventualities that may happen to us, and then being able to find an appropriate solution to our problems, at no cost to anyone.

The power behind our actions, interactions, and relationships with all things, is the deeper understanding of our purpose, and the truth behind the reasons as to why we do certain things. Once we understand the choices or decisions that we've made, we can then access our truth. For example we look for someone to love us, because we don't love ourselves or we look to others to give us security, because we feel insecure or we may work hard to please others, and we're left feeling unfulfilled. We look to others for the recognition because we hadn't recognised our own self-worth, with us experiencing low self-esteem. We then suffer from a lack of faith, belief and trust in us, which leaves us struggling in our lives, and can cause us to have no self-love.

To be truthful with ourselves is to acknowledge the unrest or disharmony within or to understand our emotional feelings. We all at times think we're ok but we're not because we don't always recognise our true feeling. When we access our truth, it's to understand what's wrong, and because of our miss-perceptions we end up deluding ourselves. It's about being accepting of what's happened to us, and embrace who we really are, being proud of us for whatever we've achieved or accomplished. We also need to accept what others have done, because we all do what we're supposed to do in order to learn from. Any outward activity could not reinstate the truth within its rightful place, as we can only do it from within.

Only when we take the inner journey, can we claim back our own power; with conviction and courage, as we realise the truth of any situation. When we have fully understood our life's purpose and lessons, our truth is what it was all about, and to what's really important to us. We need to understand our motives behind our desires; because we all strive for happiness and contentment within our lives, but not always for the right reasons. When we recognise the truth we can then achieve our goals and dreams effortlessly.

When we understand the truth, we have the knowledge that helps us on our journey through life. We need to be grateful, appreciative, and to rejoice in the glory of our lives, and of all the gracious gifts that are bestowed upon us daily, and we may have taken for granted. Our truth is about the agreement that we made before we were born; it contains all of the details into our pending lifetime. So to search for our truth would give us the information that we seek, in order to live out our lives successfully. With the help and guidance of the universal laws, we have all that we need to overcome our difficulties, from all lifetimes. Life is about living our lives to the best of our abilities, and with the natural resources that we have at our disposable.

God intended for us all to live in Peace, Harmony, and Unity, with the whole of Mankind. The problems within our lives have arisen from the emotional anguish of our souls, created by our miss-perception of the understandings of our truth. God did not create unhappiness, we did, and our unhappiness derives from the imbalances, and disharmony from within, created by thinking that we'd got it wrong, and that we're hard done too.

When we've attained our level of personal truth, we can then move onto the understanding of the truth of all existences, and what was behind the learning's. We then see a bigger picture of not just ourselves but of others too, gaining the understanding of the reasons behind our actions, and interactions. Life will always give us the mirror images and coincidences, in order to learn our lessons, but we need to learn them instantly, because we're not supposed to give our power away by struggling or by doing things needlessly. This will give us the power of our truth and energy to use within the teachings of all lives; this process goes on, until we have learned our lessons, and have become our higher conscious self once more.

When we start to see the truth, and the good within everyone, and everything, helps us with the learning's of the different situations or circumstances, and worldwide events. Our spiritual journey's takes us into the unknown territory of

17

the universal laws, the secrets behind our existence, the symbols, and hidden messages, and the inherited knowledge and wisdom. Once we recognise and activate these laws into our everyday lives, we will be living abundantly within our chosen lifestyle, living our dreams joyously, blissfully, and whole heartedly. But more importantly, we would live within the family of life, spreading our good fortune, to everyone we meet. The legacy of any lifetime is the higher vibration that is achieved from seeking the truth, and an enlightened state of awareness of the soul's continued journey.

How do we know what truth is, and how do we understand what we consider to be the truth, and be able to recognise the truth when we've achieved it? How can anyone say you're not being truthful? To be honest with ourselves and others, will help us decipher the truth, and it's every person's own responsibility to obtain, and only they will really know if they are being truthful or not, and what's really going on within their lives. Every-ones level of truth is different because of our life's experiences, and too what's already happened to us.

Our understanding of life's lessons, and to how we've actually perceived the truth behind our actions, thoughts or emotions, will enable us to access the truth of why the situation or circumstance as happened to us. If we are struggling with what is going on within our lives, then we are not being our truth. If we are finding ourselves blocked at every turn, then we are not being our truth. If we have an illness or we are feeling depressed, even that of aches and pains, then we are not being our truth, and if we do not like or even love ourselves then we are going to be unhappy with certain aspects within our lives. By not recognising what's going on within our lives, and to why we are unhappy, we have to gain the understanding in order to alleviate our problems, and instil well being.

Any disharmonious situation will denote that we're not being our truth or even if we hate getting up in a morning to go to work and so on. In fact whatever we are doing, if it's not about our highest good, and with pure intention, we end up not enjoying life to the full, and when we're not being our truth, we deceive the self. So to be content and fulfilled in all that we do is the answer, as this allows us to be in perfect harmony with life. If we enjoy what we do joyfully, we will achieve our goals or dreams at no cost to us or anyone else. For example if we hate or even resent what we're doing, then we will create pain and grief for us, mentally, physically or spiritually, and our lack of truth creates disharmony not just for us, but others too.

If we're not being honest with us or even that of an employer, partner, family or even friends, and we're unhappy about certain situations or circumstances that we find ourselves in, then we're not doing things for the right reasons. If we don't speak up for the things that we do not like or want within our lives, then we are not speaking our truth. If we don't listen to that small voice of our higher self, then we're not hearing our truth. How many times have we found ourselves doing things or even saying things just to please others, afraid of hurting them? But likewise, others would have done the same to us, and if we don't speak up for what we recognise to be our truth, then we end up denying us and others, the opportunity of becoming or recognising the truth.

To show compassion and understanding to others, and by not judging them or even ourselves, would save us all from a lot of pain and grief. If we all agreed to our lives before we came into this lifetime, and made a promise to live in our truth, in order for us all to learn from past mistakes, then none of us are wrong in what we do. We are only perceived wrongly by others or even that of ourselves; all because we didn't recognise or accept that what we're doing we were supposed to do, in order to learn from.

We must assume that at sometime or other we've all made decisions that have resulted in mistakes that may have affected others, as well as ourselves, not just in this lifetime, but in other lifetimes too. Some of the mistakes that we've made we're not going to be very proud of, but they will have

19

been part of our learning's, with us all at sometime or other having committed all of the deadly sins imaginable. In this lifetime we would only deal with the mistakes or miss judgements that we had pre-agreed too. This is known as our life's purpose, and once overcome; we would be able to reach our limitless potential, and gaining the infinite wisdom of our existence.

It is important that we live in the NOW! We have to accept all that's within our lives, because if we're unhappy with the different situations or circumstances then we're not being truthful. We have to be clear about our intentions because they will influence the outcome. We are doing what we're supposed to, as it's all part of our life's journey, so by being accepting of our situations or circumstances, will enable us to live in the now, as we spend a lot of time in the past or even projecting plans for the future, when we hadn't realised the importance of the Now, with us embracing all opportunities.

Our perception of all situations is tainted with negative traits of our learning's, and the understanding of those lessons will allow us to become our true-selves. So if we're unhappy with the person that we're living with, it's about our unhappiness, and our perception of the situation. Again the negative traits being the lessons that we need to learn. So if we love the person we're with, but are unhappy, it's because we're not being truthful with us, with regards to the unhappiness, maybe blaming the other person or even the different situations around us, when all we needed to do was recognise the unrest within, and then to heal our lives. It's human nature to blame others for our demise, especially if we don't understand our indifference to the situation or circumstances around or within us.

When blaming others is a big problem, but it's a two way street for they will blame us for their problems too, when all it needed was the both of them to sort their problems out. If we do not know what it is that we're supposed to overcome, we just get over whelmed and frustrated, even picking faults with the different things that really has no relation to what's going on or to what we're really feeling. If we are unhappy and the other person is not, this is purely about us, therefore we need to address our problems. We can look at any situation the same, whether its work, home or even in our social lives or past times. If the disharmony is evident then we need to address the situation in order to find our level of truth.

Once we have discovered or owned up to the disharmony we can then try to understand what's really going on. So if we are looking at others and their lives for example, and they are getting on with what they have chosen to do, yet we feel neglected, it's because we're not getting on with what we're supposed to be doing. Maybe picking fault with their lives helps us to self-justify why our life does not seem so interesting or that we're not living our life as it was intended.

So what is it that's lacking within our lives? It's about what we are not doing, when in fact we're supposed to be doing something for our-selves or maybe to fulfil a dream or ambition, and being accepting of the situation would allow us to feel alright about us. We put ourselves under too much pressure with us having programmed ourselves to work needlessly. Maybe we just need to recharge our batteries as our energy levels are low or we need to be still in order to listen to our bodies many needs. Because by not recognising our needs we end up denying the self, which then creates the imbalances, and disharmony within. It's our perception of the desired outcome that creates the problems especially if things don't work out as we intended, then maybe it wasn't meant to at that time, and by accepting that fact, we maintain a level of control and truth.

All of us have a life's purpose to unfold, something that we must recognise, and overcome in order to become our full potential. We must trust that when the time becomes right for us to understand all aspects of our life, we will do so. Until then just accepting what we've already achieved or accomplished, with us being proud of ourselves, will help us to

21

continue with what we're supposed to be doing. Life goes in cycles, so by not beating ourselves up, will save us from a lot of pain and grief, as soon as we start to become our truth, everything then just drops into place, and then we live in the flow of life effortlessly. We are then able to embrace life, allowing doorways to open, as the many opportunities present themselves to us, with us achieving more with less effort. We can then make real progress by connecting with the universal energies, which gives us abundance within our chosen life style, and all that we need is provided for and will come to us. The more we allow life to deliver what we need, and the more successful we become.

The answer is to do what we need to do, but to do it for us, because at times we don't recognise that we are important too. It's important that we recognise the real reason behind what we do, because by not doing so, what we desire or feel we need is blocked, and we end up denying the self. We must allow ourselves the space, and time to explore the different aspects within our lives, but also to allow others to do the same. It's about give and take, and not feeling threatened by other people's decisions or choices, and them by ours. We all have a choice; it's about being honest with us and others, listening to our inner voice, and that of our gut reaction of what's right for us. But what's right for us is not necessarily the case for others. If things are not what we want, we can change them, sometimes by just altering our perception of the situation or circumstances, and also of the people in our lives. Every person within our lives is meant to be there, for they all have something to teach us, and us them.

What we have pre-agreed too, we have chosen to do for whatever reason. Nobody has ever held a gun to our heads, and made us do anything that we didn't want to do, that is our truth, and everything that happens was meant to, and happens for a reason. We often tell ourselves, that we had no choice, when in fact we did choose; maybe helping others or doing the different things within our lives, because we thought it was expected of us, when really we didn't want too. We

22

often end up resenting them or the situation because we weren't truthful with us or maybe we'd chosen to help them, because of our own hidden agenda, sometimes being driven by our insecurities or even out of emotional blackmail. We do a lot of things in life, not realising the undertone of our actions, but whatever the case, we do what we're supposed to do, in order to play our part in accessing the understanding of our lessons. The truth is the power behind the deed or did we need to justify our actions, maybe out of guilt or even that of our pride or ego.

We all need to love ourselves with all our imperfections. Self love is important and eradicates low self esteem, disbelief, lack of faith and trust in us. Our truth and power is to have self love, belief, faith, and trust in ourselves, and to embrace our knowing thoughts, for they are our higher conscious self and intuitive responses of our truth that's within. The truth is what will set us free, and we have an obligation to us to speak our truth, to see our truth, and also to hear our truth, at all times. These are our natural inner gifts that will help us recognise our truth, in all that we do.

Clairvoyance is an inner seeing, a blind person would see with their inner vision to see what's going on around them. Clairvoyance helps us to see the things that the normal eyesight could not see, but our sixth sense makes us aware of them. This is why clairvoyance is used to see spirit and other phenomena by using the third eye, which is their inner eye.

Clairaudience is inner hearing, the inner ear that we use to hear our intuitive side, our inner voice or that of our spirit guides, guardian angels, and also our deceased loved ones. A deaf person would hear with their inner ear, hearing what they couldn't physically hear, but to hear their knowing thoughts. They would also hear or sense a vibrational force around them, because everything within our world as its own vibration, so they would be in-tune with all vibrational sounds.

Clairsentience is to sense what we cannot see or hear it's our gut reaction or instinctive ability of our intuition that leads us away from the situations that do not benefit our highest good. It's about being able to sense the vibrations around and within us that acts as an early warning that all is not well or even to instil confidence that all is well. If a person is deaf and blind, they would sense what was going on around them, and be attuned to their inner abilities and gifts.

We all have these natural gifts, skills and abilities, and they are there to enable us so we can access the truth at all times by trusting us. There really is nothing to be afraid of, nothing that is, but the projection of our personal fears, created by our ignorance that we have all that we need within, in order to access our truth, and live the life that was intended.

Everything we need is provided for; we just have to be open to receiving it, and allow our lives to change naturally and for the better. By being more self aware, and with our higher self accessing all that we need, will empower our lives with positive thoughts and actions of our truth.

CHAPTER 3

INNER JOURNEY

The inner journey of our soul's quest, what does this mean and how can we achieve it? The inner journey is the self back to the inner self, a journey that we start as soon as we are born. Throughout our early years we develop into the characters that we need to become, in order to live our chosen lifetime, successfully. Before we were born, we handpicked the situations, circumstances, and the people we chose as our parents, in order for them to perfectly match the valuable lessons that we needed to learn, and overcome throughout our lives. We do this in order for our incarnate soul to evolve successfully, and to help us to overcome the lessons of all lifetimes, with us gaining a deeper understanding to what life is really all about. We will also be given lessons from other lifetimes that are relevant to this life, and our continued growth, all being part of our life's path, with us being able to piece together the intricate details of life's tapestry that would allow our souls to evolve successfully.

Once we have lived out the major lessons within our chosen life, we start to wonder what our life has been all about. We are reasonably successful in most areas of our lives, but we may find that some aspects our lives are not quite as we expected. We may feel lost or that something is just not right, and yet we cannot quite put our finger on it. We feel that a major piece of the puzzle to our life's understanding is missing, and someone, somewhere, is withholding that vital information from us, but who?

We travel many pathways with us experiencing all walks of life, trying to find what we feel is missing within our lives. What is this mystery piece of important information that would make such a difference to us, and would help us to create Well Being, and an oneness within? Its human nature to travel outwardly trying to find what we feel is missing within our lives, yet in itself, is a great adventure and journey, because we experience many things. The lessons in life allow us to experience valuable learning that is life changing, as we travel through life. We must rejoice in the challenges and opportunities, realizing how important all lessons are, good or bad. More often than not, we focus on the negatives of life, what is lacking or what we do not have with our lives, as opposed to what we do have, this is a learned behaviour.

We are all searching for our own personal truth, unique to just us because we are all individual. The truth is hidden from us the moment we are born, and the secret is to hypothetically travel the universe in order to find it, we can take as long as we like, and can travel any pathway with whom we like, and for any reason. What we make of our lives is truly up to each individual, and there is no time scale to us reconnecting with our truth. We may even choose to stay just as we are because it gives us comfort and security or because we fear the unknown. The secret is to travel this inner journey when we feel that the time has become right, for us to do so.

So where is the truth that we seek? It's hidden deep within our hearts, and we can take a lifetime to find it, and reconnect with it once more. If we decide not to seek the truth, then we leave it all to chance, and at sometime or other we will be confronted with our life's issues in order to overcome them. If we do not embrace our lives, and seek what we feel is missing, then at the time of our deaths, our purpose and truth will be shown to us, in order for us to recognise what our life's purpose was all about. When we see the bigger picture of our lives, the understanding of what it was all about becomes clear to us, and once recognised and understood, would set us free.

We must search and find our truth whilst we're still here on the earth plane, has it would grant us with an enlightened state of existence. So when the time arrives for our passing, we would evolve to a higher plane because of our unique understanding of our life's purpose and all experiences. We all have a choice or choices to make that will play a very important part in embracing our life changing experiences. If recognised and acted upon, these experiences will place us in a blissful and fulfilling role, which makes a difference to the overall outcome for all, with us achieving Inner Peace, World Peace, Unity and Harmony.

The lack of our truth creates fear, and when we become fearful we will give away our power, with us making others or organisations, and people in powerful positions, more powerful than us. This leaves each individual struggling with their existence, not realising that by seeking and finding their truth, would in fact make them feel and be more powerful. We all at times put others down to justify how we are feeling, with us then stealing their power in order to feel better about us, but others also do likewise.

When we are content with us and our lives, we need less material wealth to survive. We then rely on our own resources, giving us an inner strength, and conviction because we know who we really are, establishing the connection to our inner gifts, skills and abilities, which we can no longer ignore or even be afraid of using. We will realise their true potential and purpose, and that they are the tools that will help us to achieve our full potential in every way, giving us back control of our everyday life and true destiny.

So our inner journey has begun. So how do we access our truth? We do this by recognising our imbalances, and the disharmony within, and eradicating it, and then re-educating us, by changing our perception to what's happened to us. When we accept responsibility for our actions, and by recognising what's wrong within our lives, we can let go of our insecurities. To acknowledge what we've done to us, and to how we've denied ourselves, we can then reinstate what we need or want back within our lives, knowing that we deserve the very best from life. We need to be honest with ourselves in order to provide for our needs and desires, and to achieve our dreams or visions. It's about being accepting of all things, and not blaming others or even the different situations or circumstances for what's wrong or missing from within our lives. We all have to stop procrastination for the hardships or thinking we'd got things wrong somehow, so by being accepting of all that happens to us, good or bad, and to look for the positives within any situation or our lives, we'll no longer judge us or others anymore.

When we can accept that everything we've done, good or bad, was in fact meant to happen, and the pathway we chose were all part of our life's learning's, and that we're meant to choose them, we end up with no regrets. Every one of us is playing our own parts in life's production in order for us all to learn from. The truth is that everyone is playing out his or her unique role of truth, within the intricate play of their lives, but hopefully with us playing the star role and not that of the understudy. So the theory is that we are all right in what we do, because we are a product of who we really are, and must accept ourselves with all our imperfections.

No one is wrong in what they do; we only perceive each other wrongly, with our perceptions being different. What we are in fact doing, is exactly what we're supposed to be doing, in order to learn, and evolve to higher aspirations, than the material gains. This will allow everyone to excel at their own pace, being tolerant and kind to others, as well as themselves. So by going within we will rediscover our true-self, it's the greatest gift anyone can give himself or herself, and it's priceless. It's the ultimate quest of connecting to our true-selves, and inner child, with us being connected to our pure essence of our inner being once more. This allows us to become who we truly are, achieving our limitless potential of all lifetimes, in order to succeed.

Meditation is very good for us, and will help us to relax, enabling us to travel inwards in order to develop our senses, and explore our inner journey of truth. This process will allow us to travel within the charka system, the body's own energy centres, with us releasing the negativity or blockages held within and at each centre. This enables us to reenergize our body's energy system, achieving Well Being, whilst caring and listening to our body's many needs, allowing the purification and cleansing of each centre. When releasing emotional trauma from within, we'll have a moment of truth of what the negative emotion was all about, allowing us to accept full responsibility for the parts we played within any situation or the different scenario's of our life's purpose.

It is important that we forgive us and others for the problems or negative experiences we've had, because it will set us free from our disharmonious situations from within. We can then rejoice for the understanding and opportunity's that we've been given, in order to learn and overcome these valuable lessons. To reconnect with our inner self, brings the mind, body, and soul back into realignment, which enables a healing on every level of existence to take place. But first we need to address an illness or disease within the required time scale, and before it's too late to reverse the illness etc. We'll then regain our health, feeling fitter, looking younger, and having more energy. If we have a disability and by reconnecting to our truth, we will be more accepting of that disability where we will realise that we can achieve all that we had hoped for, by feeling whole and complete on the inside, so it's projected to the outside of us. What we feel on the inside is what we project on the outside, this is what others see, so if we are accepting of our disabilities, so will others; they then treat us as a whole human being. If we pity ourselves, we then demand pity from others, and they will obligingly feed our negativity.

When we love, honour and respect ourselves, so will others, remember before we connected with our true selves, we look to others to provide all of our needs. But the mirror image is they will look to us also, to provide for their needs with us all putting each other under pressure. Our truth is about providing for our own needs, which means that others will not be burdened by our problems or insecurities, and then

29

in turn we will not be burdened by theirs. This will free us all, in order to take positive action in helping us to become responsible for ourselves, and getting our lives back on track. When we do this we take back the control of our everyday lives, which enables us to use our natural resources which puts less pressure on our world, and it's structure, and everyone within that structure. We then feel more content with life, because we do not have to search for ways to make us feel better or about the different aspects within our lives.

Retail therapy, holidays, fast cars, big houses or even to win the lottery are all short-term fixes for the unrest that we feel within, they would be fantastic but it's all short lived. It would make our outer world much more pleasurable but only for a short duration, and would not make us truly happy within. There is always a price to pay for external pleasures; it creates us with adventures and abundance but then we have to work to keep or maintain them, which add to the pressures of our needs or what we want within our lives. We have to be careful that we don't become a slave to our material wealth or responsibilities, and they end up controlling us, with us forgetting to enjoy the simple pleasures in life because we don't have time anymore.

The wealth that is created from within, when we have reconnected to our truth is the only wealth that will truly make us happy. There is nothing wrong with winning the lottery etc, as long as our happiness, and all aspects of our life, does not depend on it. In other words, if we had too, we could function without it. With all the natural tragedies that are happening within our world today, how would we cope if we lost loved ones, our homes, our abilities to work, in order to provide just the basic necessities? We have to rely on our natural resources within to survive, and to encourage continued growth.

We are all being put on notice to the deed, to take action into rediscovering our true selves. Then we will be in a position, in fact a greater position to the deed of evolving to the higher vibration of our highest good, and the truth of all things that would ensure Well Being on all levels of existence. When we reconnect to Mother earth, Nature, the Universal energies, and beyond will enhance our lives. The majority of us, while here on the earth plane, will never know the truth beyond our own personal truth of our inner journey, but whatever we achieve is the only real legacy that we can leave behind for our loved ones. But also, we can take that legacy with us as we continue our journey after our time on earth is over, returning back to the source from where we came a very long time ago.

The inner journey is a trip of a lifetime, the discovery of the real us is worth the effort, and demands commitment. Spirituality is not for the light-hearted, they say religious people are afraid of hell, and that spiritual people go through hell, to seek the truth. With any spiritual journey, it's about the vibrations that we expose ourselves too, allowing ourselves to be guided to the information that we need. If at first it's above our heads, so to speak, it's because for the time being we are not quite ready for that information or journey. It's about trusting our own inner guidance to seek what we need but to seek it when it's right to do so. We need to ask for what we need or desire, and it will be given to us when the time is right for us to understand or receive it, in order to help us with our continued journey and growth.

We ask many questions, and for many things, not always believing that we will receive all that we desire. The truth being, that if we do not receive that which we have asked for, it's because of timing or that we are not ready for it, in someway. But again by being accepting, we will be in control, and by not giving into the negative trait of self-punishment or even of other negative beliefs, we will maintain an element of control within our lives. It is important to stop the continuance of procrastination, because the longer we allow the negativity to go undetected, the more problems we will have to sort out in the future.

For me, the most important lesson whilst doing my inner journey was not being able to make a choice, because I was in denial of my situation and circumstances. Once I'd realised that I could make choices, I changed the things that I did not like or want within my life anymore. But first, I had to understand the significance to everything that had happened to me, but also to realise what my life had been all about. Looking back, if I had the opportunity to have known then, what I know now, would I have done things differently? The answer would be No! The difference would be that I would have still done the same things, but I would not have created the pain and grief that had for me. In hindsight, the learning's of those years actually gave me more depth to my understanding, and of my character. Just say that the time is now running out, for no one can predict the end of our world as we know it. So therefore, this is the reason that we are being put on notice to evolve, and embrace the twenty first century of the golden opportunities of the Age of Aquarius.

The Age of Aquarius will allow us all to evolve to better times; the younger generation have a lot more understanding of the importance of this evolutionary journey that we're all taking into the unknown. We are all going through a process of purification and cleansing, of the conscious and sub-conscious minds. All the information that we need is readily available to those who seek it, even though our inner journey can be quite painful, and when releasing the negative imbalances or even that of illnesses or disease can be quite stressful. By understanding the power that the mind has over the rest of the body, is an incredible insight. We don't stop to think about mind over matter, often telling ourselves that the situations that have happened to us do not matter, when in fact they do, with us taking on board, the negative effects of those thoughts or feelings, because of how we perceived them.

For me the journey was quite painful at times, but with the conviction to understand why everything had happened to me, I pushed forwards. With every new insight into how it all works, we can turn this inner journey, into an adventure. It does not matter how much personal grief we've had within our lives, just as long as we are able to alleviate a small amount of the grief or guilt, would result in us feeling better. Guilt because of the way we may have perceived the situation in the first place, and grief because of the procrastination of thinking that we were to blame in some-way or that we could have done more to help. By being accepting of all that happens to us, saves us time and pain, and once I recognised where I had stored that pain, I released it and then forgave myself for what I'd done to me. Once I had understood the significance of that pain, I then released the imbalances from within, and Well Being was restored. At times I felt stupid, disbelieving how I could have allowed the unrest to happen in the first place, but in hindsight, if we are not aware of what we are actually doing to the physical body or mind, then we cannot protect ourselves from us.

The inner journey is about recognising our truth about any given situation, then having the conviction to only do the things that are about our highest good, and only having our best interests to heart, as well as everyone else's. Because in standing up for what we believe, will not only put us on the right pathway, but will allow others to do the same. We all at times, just go along with the different situations to please others, not always for the right reasons.

So for me, I did a lot of people pleasing, doing the things that I did, firstly to fulfil certain voids within me, and secondly because I needed to be loved and to have my self-worth recognised. But we must understand is that we would have done these things anyway, because they were a big part of the lessons that we needed to learn from. With all things that we do in life, we should have done them in a positive way, and for the right reasons, without the negative underlining cause influencing the outcome. If I was connected to my higher self in the first place, I would not have created the negativities within that come from the lower emotional physical self, having created the illusions of my interpretation of what my life was all about. Remember, to feel insecure or to have any emotional issues within, makes us do things for the wrong reasons. So we need to rejoice the opportunities that life presents to us, in order to understand our life's purpose, and allow us to complete the cycle of rediscovering our true essence, of our inner-self and truth. This is the truth about our actions, and interactions within all aspects of our lives, and is life changing.

We all at times, find it overpowering and very miss-leading, having spent the best part of our lives oblivious of what we have done to us, and the journey of the enlightened self. Was this information deliberately kept from us? The well kept secrets that would have set us free, and the information that we'd kept from us because of our fears. Once we'd understood what our fears were all about, allows us to achieve all that we desire effortlessly. It would be great to be in the position of connecting to the power of our truth, with us being able to enjoy life to the full, and not having to wait for some divine order to wave its magic wand, and set us free. The only true miracle is the one we give to us, by being more open to our own power of intention, and with courage and conviction, can reclaim back our personal truth. With the reconnection with the universal energies of our creator that's found deep within us, we would have the power of our truth guiding us forwards. This process enables us to reconnect with the ultimate power of the universe, and that of the universal gifts, skills and abilities of all lifetimes, this enables us to achieve our limitless potential.

For some they will dismiss their unique gifts as nonsense, maybe thinking they've made it this far without any divine intervention, and that they don't exist for them anyway. Some people think that these gifts are only for the selected few or even just for people who have their heads stuck in the clouds. Over the years I have found people not really being comfortable with what I did spiritually or even with the understanding of the unknown, and I often found myself judged wrongly. But who's to say that it's only now become the right time for us all to know more about our hidden abilities, and the mystical wonders of our incredible world. No one that is, but each individual. But through fear, pride and the ego, we will be kept in the dark to these unique qualities, which could reinstate peace and harmony within every aspect of our lives. Some people thinking it is the dark side of nature to experience the paranormal, but if it brings us into the light, how can it be wrong, remember opposites attract.

The inner journey is the ultimate state of awareness of the real us. Maybe at first experiencing our own inner fears and of the unknown, but once these as been alleviated they will be our guide and life saver. The emotion of fear is a positive emotion, and would lead us away from danger; it cannot lead us into danger unless we ignore the warning, and if we had not fully appreciated the true meaning of its importance. To be fearful, means that something awful may, or may not happen, to be fearless is to be brave, but that does not mean we are invincible.

To have fear means that something may be pending, it does not mean that it will definitely happen. The strong emotion of fear leads us away from danger, not into it. If we are afraid of fear we multiply our negative emotions, which will then create paranoia tendencies, and can bring the negative situations into our lives. We can then conjuror all sorts of demons from the past, all of which are created by our own imaginations and fears. If these fears are allowed to go undetected, along with our miss-interpretation of our perceptions of our imbalances, beliefs and concepts of how we think it all are. We will consequently cause ourselves to be fearful of living our lives to the full, by not allowing ourselves to appreciate our lives as it should be, and to be more accepting of all things that we do have within our lives, because if not we end up deluding us.

During the completion of our soul's inner journey, there is nothing to fear, it's a natural process. We must have trust, faith, and belief that our best interests are always a priority of the universe. By accessing our higher consciousness is for the sole intention of everyone's rightful place within the kingdom of our source, and reconnecting to the power of creation with us having the whole of the universe at our disposal.

The inner journey of The Essential Creativity of Awareness is a journey where we can rediscover our essential self, true-self and truth, once more. We can reconnect with our creative abilities of our inner gifts that speak to our heart and soul but also makes us aware of all that's within our lives, both good and bad. We need to be able to fully appreciate the real us, giving ourselves the chance to be able to live life just for us, as was intended. We do this by accessing the unconditional forces of our inner and true self, which activates our higher consciousness which puts us in a strong position of achieving our limitless potential.

When we're able to understand our true inner-self, the person we have always aspired to be, and the person we'd forgotten all about. The inner self is the power behind our thoughts and deeds, and is our higher conscious self. We have always been free to make our choices in life, and the choices that we've made, were all part of the divine plan. Our life's journey is to see if we can successfully reconnect with the true vibration of our higher conscious self once more, because we'd disconnected from the real us, a very long time ago, through the negative traits of our emotions, and miss-understandings how we'd perceived our lives to be. Through free will, and the power to just be ourselves, we can all claim back the unique power of us that will allows us all to have the life that was always intended.

CHAPTER 4

HOLISTIC GIFTS, SKILLS & ABILITIES

We are now living in the golden Age of Aquarius, where holistic techniques and the spiritual phenomena, along with paranormal investigations are more readily accepted, no longer being perused behind closed doors for the selected few. The unknown was often frowned upon as the occult, fearing supernatural experiences as the work of the devil. All of our natural spiritual abilities and gifts are in fact our own unique tools of our higher consciousness, presenting them to us when we need help in understanding the unknown, the unseen life force, and the energy that connects all of creation, pulsating throughout our planet, the universe and beyond. This unique energy also pulsates within and around our physical bodies, feeding our lower consciousness, and helps us with the transition to our higher conscious self, enabling us to complete our obligation of the self, with the reconnection of all things encompassing.

Holistic techniques, and our gifts, skills, and abilities, what are they? They are the tools of the trade, the tools that can help us all on our spiritual journey, but using these tools with our own natural abilities or spiritual gifts which will enable us with self-healing. Holistic techniques are about the healing of the whole person, the mind, body, and soul, and not just the symptoms of the illness or disease. Natural healing happens when we understand why we have a medical problem, sometimes we have just the symptoms, but if ignored they become a condition. When we understand the imbalances within we can successfully rectify the problem by our own healing powers, as long as the reason or reasons behind the problem is diagnosed first.

These problems are our body's unique way of telling us that there is an imbalance within and needs attention. If these problems go undetected they will develop, into a condition, and then eventually into a disease. The word disease is as it says, dis-ease; it's about something we are not happy with, and is causing unrest within. As I've already said, everything that happens to us happens for a reason, so we owe it to ourselves firstly to seek medical help, but also to administer self-help, holistic remedies, therapy or any holistic technique to elevate the condition.

It is quite safe for us to administer alternative therapies alongside our conventional ways, maybe advising our medical practitioner of our intention, so that when the problems are located, diagnosed and understood, we are then healed on a physical, emotional, mental, spiritual, and also the soul level as well. Inner guidance is about listening to the small voice within; the message given that if acted upon would lead us away from danger or would detect an illness or symptom, preventing us from causing unnecessary pain or grief. Being attuned to our body, is also a way of detecting the imbalance, and disharmonies sooner rather than later, by paying attention to our gut feelings, intuitive reactions or inner guidance.

The Essential Creativity of Awareness is about us having a responsibility to ourselves, and to become aware of our bodies many needs, and then unleashing our potential to alleviate the unrest within.

It is ESSENTIAL that we do everything within our power to overcome and provide for our bodies many needs, making it our priority and not putting off until tomorrow, that which we can be achieved today. The sooner we all understand, and rectify the disharmony or imbalances within and around us, we can then learn the lessons that will connects us to our higher consciousness, and allow us to open up to our creative side, which will unleash our unique gifts.

The CREATIVITY of our being allows us to explore all the different techniques that are available to us. This allows us to open our minds, and expand our minds energy, in order to be aware of our creative self. We then unleash our natural gifts, skills, and talents that will allow us to be more creative within our everyday lives. We need to take our responsibilities more seriously, realising that if we've created an illness in the first place, we can then make it better by using our unique gift of self-healing. If we came into this life with a disease or illness already in place, we have to make sure that we learn the lessons or the reason why we have the condition, but to learn it on a deep fundamental level, to ensure the overall lesson and healing, takes place successfully and on a soul level. Miracles do happen, where people have truly recovered, with no trace of the disease or condition, and no explanation other than a life changing experience or altered state of awareness has occurred. This happens with us altering our perception of how we thought things were, to how things really are, and maybe the illness was an illusion or just a part of the learning or understanding of our life's lessons and purpose.

Sometimes an illness or disease can come from another lifetime brought into this one, just waiting for us to learn the lesson associated with it. It's about understanding what we've done to us, and also about us being healed on every level, including that of the soul level, which would help with the healing of any past lifetime's illness or disease, and any other disharmonious situation. To have creativity is to be able to enjoy these precious gifts by opening up to them, giving us back the power to do things within our lives that we'd only been dreaming of. When we're living our dreams it brings out the creative side of us, allowing our natural talents, skills, and abilities, to be expressed in all that we do, and allow us to reawaken our creative nature. There have been cases where people have found themselves being able to paint or play music, not having realised that they were gifted. To become creative, we express ourselves on the deeper fundamental levels, in ways that we could not otherwise do, if we were not connected to our true self.

Our AWARENESS is about us taking more notice of what is going on around and within us, first becoming aware of ourselves, and our feelings, thoughts, actions and interactions with us and others. We start sensing the vibrations of the different circumstances and situations, giving us more insight into the imbalances and disharmony within. But also helping us sense the positive vibrations of the solutions needed, and what is expected of us, making us more aware of the earth and universal energies.

We then begin to be aware of the different places and vibrations, picking up happiness, sadness or even some tragic event. The different vibrational influences that we start to sense can leave us feeling in awe, and at times leaving us very uplifted or we may feel physically drained. It's also about protection of the self, to the different vibrations that we attract, because until we understand them, and able to appreciate their true meanings they can affect us.

We need to be in control of us and protect our energy field, as we pick up on the different situations that we cannot hear or even see, but that we sense. This is when fear sets in, because if we cannot see, hear or feel it, we tell ourselves it doesn't exist, but we are sensing something, maybe becoming fearful of the unknown. We can pick up fears of others and their situations or even just to allow our own fears to multiply out of our anxiety of not recognising the illusions of life. Once we overcome our fears, we will relax and actually enjoy this new found state of awareness.

To be aware of the mind, body and soul, the mental, physical and spiritual, will enhance our lives in such a way that we will enjoy travelling the universe and back again, in search for our hidden truth. It's a journey that will take us to the magical places and realms, where all we desire can be manifested. Reconnecting us to all the positive attributes of long ago, to reconnect with ourselves is surely the best thing that we will ever do, with us reconnected to our higher consciousness, and our true-self once more. So by opening up to all the different aspects of our lives we will enhance them. We experience a lot of different cultures, using the different techniques that will broaden our outlook, not just of this lifetime, but of all lifetimes, reconnecting to our planet, the universe and the creator of all that is.

To be reconnected to the fountain of wisdom, everything that we need can be obtained from our wealth of knowledge which then gives us the infinite wisdom. When we look back in the scriptures, we see that a visible halo was around the top of people's heads. These halo's represent our higher conscious vibrations, and conscious awareness, with us being pure in every way. But over the centuries, and through the trials and tribulations of life, and after taking on board, more and more negativity, has resulted in us becoming unattached from our higher consciousness. Thus making our HALO'S no longer visible, to the naked eye.

When we have successfully connected to our higher consciousness and ascended state, we can actively start the process of climbing the spiritual ladder to raise our vibrations to the point where our aura's will actually glow and radiate positive energy and colour, which can be seen by those who can see aura's with the naked eye. Very few people have been called saints, but there are such people in our world today, who have halos, but we have to be highly evolved to be able to see someone's halo. To be honest, I do not think that anyone in today's world as we know it could see these halos, but in the future and after we have evolved, who knows! I believe that in heaven, and once we'd conquered our soul's quest, we would be able to see this magnificent sight.

Nature is a great healer, so by just stepping outside allows us to enjoy its beauty, to see its magnificence and all its glory in unity. The forces of nature show us our strengths and weaknesses, nature just flows with energy as it completes cycles, evolving over centuries, and is influenced by the universal and cosmic vibrations. We are all a big part of nature, as we go through the different stages of growth and cycles. When we connect with nature it brings unity of humankind, in order for us to understand the importance of

41

our exposure to this incredible life force. Nature feeds our minds, bodies and souls, exposing us to the different minerals and nutrients that are important to our growth and well being. Also we need exposure to the different elements such as wood, fire, water, earth and metal, and their association with creation, and balance and harmony of all things, again important to our well being.

The flowers, trees and vegetation, with all their unique properties, in fact everything we need to survive whilst on our planet. The understanding of unity creates an abundance of wealth and prosperity, and all that we need is provided for us by the universe, mother earth, and nature, supporting the animal kingdom and mankind. All that is asked of us is to respect, honour, and worship these simple but essential gifts that are given abundantly, and once recognised and appreciated will aid us in achieving a well being state.

The wind blows our cobwebs away allowing us to clear our heads, as the wind gently creases our energy field, helping us to release negativity or blockages from within. Water cleanses our auras and also our physical bodies, allowing us to reshape our thoughts, and with reprogramming we can let go of all that we no longer want or need. The colours and textures of nature, gives us structure to our existence, they are uplifting and pleasing to the eye, our touch or smell, tantalising our senses. The vast space that nature creates by stepping outdoors, will give us freedom from the restraints and restrictions of our problems. With fresh air expanding our lungs and minds, will enhance clear thinking, enabling us to be at one with ourselves and nature, which connects us to our creator, and the solutions to our problems can be achieved.

We all have spiritual guides, guardian angels and spiritual helpers with us, who are they, and why do they draw near? There is a lot of trepidation about the spiritual world, no one can prove of its existence but neither can they prove that it doesn't exist, so my philosophy is, if it does not exist, it cannot hurt or harm us in any way, and if it does exist, it did not harm us when we were not aware of its existence, so why would it hurt or harm us, when we learn of its existence. The only ways it can harm us is by our own perception of it, and where fear knows no boundaries.

A Spirit Guides help us to overcome our learning's within this lifetime, and we are a fragmentation of them. In other incarnate lives we were highly evolved and achieved great things, so our spiritual guides hold within them the important aspects of us, and also the understanding of our learning's. They also help us to access the secrets of mankind, and the universe, in achieving our enlightened status. As we grow and evolve, they continue to inspire and encourage us forwards with the quest of our souls. Over our lifetime we will have a lots of different spirit guides with us, helping us to continue the cycle of evolution. On the earth plane, we also meet different spiritual earth teachers, who pass on the important information that we need in order to understand our life's purpose. These earth teachers are part of our soul groups, and we meet and communicate with them through the different incarnate lifetimes that we have because they had pre-agreed to help us. The deeper our levels of understanding of life's experiences, the more knowledge and wisdom we gain, making us more accepting of the unknown.

A Guardian Angel is someone assigned to us from birth, and they only have our best interests at heart. They look after us, and guide through our most difficult times, encouraging us onwards because they are the inner voice within us. Angels really do exist, and we can ask them to prove it by showing us a sign or delivering us a feather that really does come from nowhere, because they really do watch over and protect us.

Our Spiritual helpers are sometimes our loved ones that have passed over, some we may have met on the earth plane, others we just know of, but whatever the case they draw close to offer comfort, love and support. Never judging us, but like us, they still have lessons to learn, maybe just a continuance of a lesson they did not fully understand whilst still here on the earth plane. But a lesson that if learned, would have a positive knock on effect for all concerned, these are the positive attributes of their existence. Fortune telling can be very misleading because its sole purpose is to let you know of the continuance of life after death, but not in the way we know it here on the earth plane. But to prove to us that the spirit does live on, sometimes we have readings hoping that our spirit friends can advise us or wave a magic wand to make our lives better. But this is not what it's about, what we are being told hypothetically is what we want to hear, but deep within us we already know the answers to our problems.

A Great Medium gives us evidence to the survival of death, by describing our loved ones with information that they could not possibly have known about the person, yet giving us comfort and words of assurance that life really does go on. They give us the infinite knowledge and wisdom of their existence, and offer continued support that they have always shown to us, and will continue to give us, even after their death. But whatever lessons we have to learn, so do them, a continuance of our soul's quest.

There are a lot of holistic techniques available to us, in order to become more aware of our many needs. Our natural gifts, skills, and abilities, along with our beliefs, and the different remedies help us to connect us with our divine self. In other words any holistic technique that acts as a channel from our lower consciousness, and physical self, to our divine or higher consciousness.

These techniques allow us to explore the mystical realms, decoding the secrets to our hidden messages, and too understanding the symbolism of their true meanings. This enables us to reconnect with the collective consciousness, and reach an enlightened state of awareness. Once we had successfully reconnected to our higher conscious self, we would not need any holistic tool to help us heal our lives, and with the continuance of our connection to the higher realms.

Because these tools are only used as a focus, we do not actually need any of them, other than the commitment to our higher conscious self, as the holistic tools act as a bridge, from our lower conscious self, to our higher conscious self, and the universal and divine energies.

Our reconnection with these powerful energies will allow us to maintain our level of truth, and connect us to self faith, belief and trust in us, and of all that we need. Our own unique gifts and abilities that once understood and reactivated, would become our own healing attributes, and our reconnection to our source, and the constant supply of the universal energies. This energy would cleanse and purify our mind, bodies, and soul, and keeps us connected to mother earth, which helps us to keep grounded at all times, in order to build a firm foundation on which to build our earthly lives upon. This enables us to activate all that we need in order to live abundantly, within our chosen life styles. It's important that we recognise that any past time pursuits could also be used to achieve a well being state. Such as music, art, in fact any creative hobby or even career, all having a positive benefit if pursued in the right way, and for the right reasons.

The holistic therapy that I enjoyed the most, and thought to be the most beneficial, was the art of Kinesiology. It helped me to achieve more in a short space of time, than all the other holistic techniques put together, but this is my own personal choice. Kinesiology is the art of muscle testing, a direct response to a problem or condition, whilst working with the higher consciousness. We used charts of information that would help us to decipher the hidden truth of our higher self, and then administered remedies, or affirmations which would help with the realignment of our energy field, and the different organs or source points, throughout the physical body. We would unlock the negativities and blockages, even those of ailments, illness or diseases, from the mental, physical, emotional, and spiritual bodies, giving healing on a soul level, and beyond. We would deal with problems from present day, being regressed through the years to childhood, conception,

45

and past lifetimes, its uniqueness giving a deeper fundamental learning's to all lives.

I have personally enjoyed the various holistic techniques and understanding of their cultures, such as Aromatherapy, Reflexology, even that of Acupuncture, again healing of the mind, body and soul. I found Homoeopathic Flower, and Herbal remedies very effective, they have been used for thousands upon thousands of years, healing the physical, mental, emotional, and spiritual levels of a person. They uplift the spirit so we can begin with the healing process; these remedies play a big part in the understanding of the different ailments and conditions, but also in helping us overcome our own personal role of self-help.

It's about belief in ourselves and our abilities, but also having belief, faith, and trust in us, and the universe, which then as a major effect on all that we do. The remedies help us when we're feeling out of balance, but we don't know the cause or reason as to why? The remedies gently bring to the surface the disharmonious situations or emotional beliefs, where they can be dealt with, and healed.

I have also used Angel cards, Tarot cards and Rune stones; they were excellent for inner guidance, helping to understand the reasons of the negative problems, ailments or to the different conditions or circumstances. They were also very useful in the realignment of the mind, body and soul, and can attune us to our sixth sense whilst in meditation, also in communication with the spirit world, bringing comfort and healing. Crystals and colour also played a big part in my inner journey, again giving healing from the different qualities of the crystals and there colours, inducing balance and harmony of the mind, body or soul. The importance of colour in our everyday lives, gives us strength, vitality and healing. We can tell a lot about a person by what colour clothes they are wearing on a daily basis.

I enjoyed working directly with spirit, the different spirit guides, and guardian angels, and departed loved ones. They brought not only guidance and comfort, but an insight into the mysteries of the continuance of life after death, but also the eternal evolution of our existence, from when time began. The magical wonders of the unknown is to enable us all to be more self aware, and to know that by lifting our vibrations to an higher conscious state, an healing takes place that needs no remedies, holistic techniques, or culture. Miracles really do happen but we have to believe in them, and also that we are worthy of a miracle, should we need one. All it takes is just the belief in our higher conscious self, and the exposure of the divine, and the universal energies that have sustained all life and our universe, since time began.

Meditation was for me a very beneficial, because without the art of meditation, the doorway to my higher self would not have been easy to reach. We need to be in a relaxed meditative state where we can release stress or tension. Meditation is the stairway to our higher consciousness; it has an abundance of positive benefits that allow us to be more relaxed, and gives us an abundance of energy that encourages us to take our lives more in our stride, enabling us, to become less stressed.

This process of meditation elevates stress or tension, giving us the positive qualities needed in order to eradicate illness or disease. Meditation helps us with the journey of self-awareness, allowing us to become more attuned to our minds, body's and souls, helping us to sort the inner disharmony, and imbalances, by reconnecting us with the truth and inner us. This allows us to be more aware of our natural gifts, skills, and abilities, giving us the opportunity to understand our own unique healing abilities, and all that we need to survive within the structure of our world.

I have enjoyed the communication with the spirit world, the healing messages, and the guidance of spirituality, also being able to encourage others to draw their loved ones closer to them, so they too, could experience the realms of love and continued support. The communication with their loved ones, and spiritual guides, allowed them to also reconnect with the angelic realms of the angels. This also helped them to become more aware of themselves, and in healing their lives, so they too could reconnect to their true selves, and that of their truth once more. This gave them access to their unique gifts, skills, and abilities, allowing them the opportunity to understand the importance of these wondrous gifts, and living their lives to the full. The Workshops that I ran were with the sole intention for each individual to understand what was going on within their own lives. We are so close to our problems at times that we really do forget to help the self.

The classes were designed for interaction between like-minded people; it helped them to realise that they were not the only ones, struggling with the lessons in life. We always started the class with a meditation, bringing our spirit guides, and guardian angels closer to us, helping to channel the divine and universal energies, and opening us up to receiving the healing vibrations, allowing our natural healing abilities to do their work. It also helped them be exposed to the higher vibrations of the collective vibration of mankind, with us all working as a team, in order to help one another. This helped us all to understand our problems or disharmony and the imbalances within because by helping others we help us to achieve a well being state.

The workshops were designed and enabled me to cover a wide range of spiritual subjects, giving a taster into the insights of the unknown. What people enjoyed the most were the communication, and the input from others, along with the advice, and the support that they needed in believing in themselves. The encouragement that they all showed to one another gave them confidence in their own abilities. The interaction that they had with each other, allowed them to see the mirror images of life, it proved to them how everything they needed was provided for. It enabled them to recognise what they sought came from the different situations, circumstances, people, and from unexpected sources, and they were left in awe of how simple the solutions to their problems were easy to recognise, realising that there was nothing to fear.

The unknown is always feared, but with respect and proper guidance to the different aspects of the spiritual phenomena, no harm ever came to them, and once they'd understood how unique their gifts were, they enjoyed exploring their potential. Each and every-one of us will use our gifts differently, with us putting our take on how we perceive them which makes us all unique and individual. The more that they used their gifts the more they understood how powerful they were, and too what could be achieved, they were amazed to how simple it was to attain the solutions to their problems.

Common sense was often the order of the day because at times the solution was so easy that they found they'd always known the answer to their problem, but was afraid to voice it, because the solution seemed too simple in relation to the situation they found themselves in. The answers to our problems are always staring us in the face, the reason being, the lessons that we needed to learn in this lifetime we'd already been pre-programmed with the solutions, held within the sub conscious, that small voice within. By altering the way we view the different situations, and with reconnection to the higher vibration, give us access to the answers. The desired outcome will then have an impact on us, leaving us wanting to know more, and enables us to put it into practice what we have learned every-day.

I have enjoyed being with like-minded souls, reading lots of self-help books, and also meeting different people from all walks of life along the way. I've also enjoyed hours of discussions on the numerous theories, and debates, covering a wide range of subjects on paranormal activities, all of which played a big part in the journey of my soul's quest. Most of all, I have enjoyed the communication, and the interaction of sharing the infinite knowledge and wisdom with all who came into my life. There is no new knowledge and wisdom for all is ancient and infinite, and the pleasures and joy in life is gathering that knowledge and wisdom together. This information is the legacy of truth, and it's important that we pass on this legacy to all we meet whilst still here on the earth plane, and is the only true legacy that we get to take with us, on our infinite journey of the continuance of our soul's quest.

CHAPTER 5

AWAKENING TO OUR DREAMS

We travel many pathways in search of our truth, with us achieving a lot of our ambition's, goals, desires and dreams along the way. Some of us will have bought up our own families, watching them too, start their own journeys in searching for similar goals or ambitions. We all have hobbies, skills, and abilities, and different vocations, views, beliefs, and come from different backgrounds, which shape our unique characters making us all individual. We have one common goal, and that's to fulfil our dreams, as we travel the different pathways in search of our purpose, and hopefully enjoying all of life's experiences.

We will not find what we are looking for outside of ourselves, only by reconnecting with our inner self, and the essence of our true spirit, will we be able to fulfil our dreams by manifesting them consciously. We do this by reawakening to our dreams or goals, and they happen easily when we've reconnected with our higher conscious self, in order to tap into our limitless potential. Our dreams are memories of long ago, and in other incarnate lifetimes, where we successfully achieved them.

Our dreams are what we naturally aspire too, because of their enjoyment or the fulfilment that they gave us long ago. Or they may of been the dreams of our pastimes or vocations that we'd achieved or accomplished, maybe making us materially or financially rich, and left us feeling fulfilled and content within our lives. The memory of these accomplishments makes us aspire to repeating them again, in other incarnate lives, when we have successfully completed our life's purpose and lessons. The soul's quest is to reawaken to these memories of long ago, allowing us to achieve our dreams once more.

We all need to be our truth in order to accomplish our dreams; we need to accept everything that we have within our lives, as this helps us to appreciate how lucky we already are, and helps us to recognise that we're already living part of our dreams. We all hold a vision of what we want to accomplish, not realising that the process of accomplishing our vision is also part of achieving our dreams. So by living in the now, allows us to be fully in our lives, and everything that we do have, we are meant to have them, with us seizing opportunities whole heartedly. With every step we take, we get closer to achieving those dreams and all that we desire. It's important that all we do is for our highest good and that of everyone concerned. Because enjoying all that we do every-day, gives our lives a whole new dimension, with us playing the star role in the production of our life. We must surrender totally, going with the flow of life, and being fully accepting of all things, realising that our dreams are an extension of us, and our truth.

We must all aspire to the knowledge that we are worthy of great things, and we must give ourselves permission to only attracted the very best from our lives, because in doing so, we are effectively saying that we are worth it. At times the outside pressures within our lives, make things very difficult for us to achieve what we want, and they cloud the issues that's then creates the unrest within, stopping us from achieving our dreams.

With life's struggles and after trying to achieve what we desire, we often give up, maybe out of disillusionment because things haven't gone to plan. We then try something new or alter our perception of what we're doing, thinking that it will be different next time, if we try again. We always think the grass is greener until we jump; only to find we are blocked yet again. What we do not realise is, that it's us that's doing the blocking, and at times self-sabotage our efforts, why would we do this? Sometimes out of frustration, disappointment, insecurity, or even resentment, with us thinking that life was treating us harshly or we're being punished in some-way. We often wonder why these things happen to us, and because we hadn't faced our insecurities or disharmony within, we'd unknowingly put obstacles in our way, justifying that we knew it wouldn't work out anyway, and giving us a reason as to why.

So why is it so difficult to achieve our dreams? Maybe because of the timing, maybe the time was not right? Or that we had not fully understood our learning's. Maybe we still had things to overcome, and by not realising that fact, we find life a struggle. We never really appreciate what we have within our lives, unless we worked hard to achieve it. By not accepting these things as being part of the divine, and procrastinating, we'll delay our dreams by creating the imbalances within our everyday lives. It's recognising that we do in fact achieve things because we are striving to achieve our dreams, by taking small steps every-day to fulfilling our dreams. We make the choices that we do, in order to help us to grow, but more importantly, to help in attaining the deeper knowledge and understanding of our truth, which will set us free, and helps us with our dreams. So it's worth the hard work, and the understanding, because we'll realise that we do desire the best that life can offer, but more importantly we'll realise that we've kept us in the dark, with the illusions of life.

Our dreams are just that, our dreams, we can only put them into reality when we have understood our lessons. Every-day in every-way we work to achieving those dreams, not knowing that they don't come into fruition until the time is right for them to do; this is why we get so frustrated with us. Our dreams are the memories of positive events that happened long ago, they are a series of scenes in our minds whilst in our sleeping or waking states. We hypothetically have been in a sleeping state, waiting for the time to become right in order for us to wake up, to our truth and dreams. To reawaken to our truth, by being true to ourselves once more, and too the promises we made to fulfil our dreams. It's about the things that we want within our lives, and to why we want them? It's not about doing things, just to prove to others that we are successful, it's about the doing them because we want to and to do it with a passion, as we need to be passionate about our lives.

When accomplishing our dreams we need to recognise what needs to be done, and push aside any setbacks. In other words to look at any blocks that's stopping us from moving forwards, and in understanding them, we can push them aside in order to get on with the job in hand. We need to recognise the opportunities in life, and they will help us with the understanding of how to achieve our dreams effortlessly, and to fulfil our life's purpose, will then in turn, help us realise our limitless potential and that of achieving it. To be fully in our lives, and to just go with the flow of life, will enable us to be accepting of all that's within our lives. When we are connected to mother earth, the universal energy, and to the unity of mankind, we can achieve all that we want, but on a higher level of consciousness. This is when our dreams become a reality.

In our dream states we are given the memories of our agreement which we made to ourselves before we came to this lifetime. When we understand our dreams or memories the illusions of life just drift away, making us realise that what we're left with, is our own power of intention, with us seeing and wanting our dreams for the right reasons. Because we all go through life at times chasing rainbows, thinking if we could just reach that pot of gold at the end of it, then life would be so much better. The only rainbow to chase is the one within, our own unique chakra system; with the seven primaries colours, playing there part in helping us achieve balance and harmony, of the mind, body, and soul. The pot of gold is found within our heart, and connected with God, our life force energy, and the secrets of mankind, and most of all to our own personal power of divinity, where dreams really do come true, and miracles are performed.

Our lives feel like we have been in a dream, waiting to wake up, and for some they will say they have been living a nightmare, a life with so much pain and grief. We can make life very hard for ourselves at times, always trying to achieve our goals but at times they are just out of reach or we have pushed them away, with us then moving onto something else. We live in the past at times or even the future, and very rarely in the now! Never really feeling content, but to live in the now, we'd stand more chance of achieving our dreams. Instead of wishing we could roll back the years or go to a time when life was much better, wanting to recapture some idyllic memory of when we thought we were happier. We must be careful that we don't wish our lives away; by thinking that if we could only move forwards, we would have better times. It's strange how at times we think we would be happier in different situations or circumstances but that's never the case, because the disharmony within, would reflect the disharmony without. When we move from one thing to the next, doesn't solve the disharmony either, it only adds to our unrest, because until we deal with our disharmony we'd take it with us wherever, and whatever we do.

When we chase our dreams before our intentions are really clear, makes us lose faith in ourselves, creating doubts within, with us then dreaming about what made us happy in the past, or even thinking what would make us happy in the future. Dealing with our problems in the now will keep us focused on today, where we stand more chance of changing our lives for the better. The present time is a where we can be more carefree, and have more personal time to be able to appreciate the simple pleasures of life; and rejoice, sharing laughter and joy, giving us more fun times together. When living our dreams we feel we can achieve anything we want, and as long as we are true to ourselves, and not trying to please others or to be something we're not.

We live in a world where we are not judged for ourselves, but for all we have. We must be careful that we don't follow the path of necessity where our wealth controls us, and not us controlling our wealth. Sometimes we have to work hard to maintain our life styles, and then we don't have time to fulfil our dreams and desires anymore or even to enjoy them. We must live our lives the best way we can, because of the extra pressures that we put ourselves under at times. We must always remember to enjoy the different experiences of the adventures of life, as they can be very rewarding. But at times we will realise that something is still missing within our lives, and it's the promise we made to us to fulfil our purpose in life, and achieve all that we desire consciously.

The thing we notice most when we are busy pursuing our purpose, is a lack of time, as we have no time to do what we really want to do, maybe just to have more time to do nothing, and relax. When we feel the pressures of our expectations, of the choices we've made, they weigh heavy upon us. We then feel the hardships of life, often telling ourselves that we have nothing to fret about, because there is always someone, worse off than us, so we feel we shouldn't complain. It's important to recognise our hardships and need to be overcome. By not focusing on the latter, it will only bring us discontentment within our lives.

There comes a time in everyone's life, and if the opportunity is recognised and acted upon, will change our life forever, it's about us recognising what is really important, our family and vocation, maybe also enjoying good health because we can't take it for granted. Good health as to be worked on, it's about slowing down, allowing us the opportunity to hear that small voice within that speaks to us, and helping us to overcome and understand our lessons in life, which helps us to achieve our dreams. What are dreams made of? They are made from our creative abilities and talents, allowing us to achieve the uniqueness of our true selves; they are the things that are really a part of our higher conscious self, and things that come naturally to us. Not necessarily something we learn, but something that we do without thinking about, but they give us a great deal of pleasure, satisfaction, and fulfilment to us.

The knowledge and wisdom, and everything we want to accomplish sounds so easy to achieve, but to put it into action

56

is a different thing, we hear what we are being told, but how does it really work? When we detach ourselves from our lives, we can then take an honest look to see what is really happening within, and around us. With a clear view, we will instinctively know what we'd like to achieve, but when we get confused by what we want to achieve, we'll tell us it's unachievable or not possible. We then find other things getting in the way of us achieving our dreams. We'll try time and time again, to put our dreams and desires into action, but its hard work, as nothing seems to flow, why? It's because we're not doing things for the right reasons or we're not in a position that would enable us to make a decision based on our truth. It's by connecting with our inner self that gives us access to our truth, which then gives us the vital information that is needed in order to make the right decisions.

To achieve our dreams, the reasons why we want them must be pure, and if we thought they would just make us feel better then they will not enhance our lives. Our dreams are just that, our dreams, but wanting them for the wrong reasons, actually push them away. No matter what our dreams are, if we wanted then in order to run away from our emotional feelings, situations or insecurities, with us thinking that we'd be happier, then we'd want them for the wrong reasons. To fulfil our dreams we have to acknowledge that our intention is to become our true-self, in order to achieve our purpose in life. With us being able to enjoy what we've achieved with a passion of true intention, and not just making us materially rich. Our desires and dreams, cannot in anyway, be intended to fulfil the negative emotions or voids, which we feel within. Or even to give us the recognition that we crave maybe of self-worth or even to feed our pride and ego. Our dreams can only come into fruition when we have reconnected to the inner self and that of our truth, and then we're able to live out our dreams when the time becomes right for us to do so. Until then we pursue our desires, enjoying every aspect of our lives, making progress with the view to successfully overcome our lessons. This gives us much more control over our everyday lives, realising that we are doing exactly what we are

57

supposed to be doing. But to be doing them joyfully, enjoying every day, and every experience as thou it was our last. To fulfil our dreams, is by reawakening to the fact that deep within us, is the essence of the memories of all that we have achieved or accomplished long ago. These memories will enable us to reach our full potential, to enrich our lives with all of the gifts and abilities that derive from our talents. We then experience our natural state of creativity that helps us to attain success in all we do.

The number one dream is to win the lottery; we believe it would improve everything within our lives. We would not have to work; we could live in a big house, or even take the holidays that we had dreamed of, have a great car and so on. We tell ourselves that we would be able to help those people closest to us, or even to give to a good cause. But the truth is, it would not give us what we truly want, because all of those things, have just a short term benefit, and we would soon find ourselves, back to square one. We only have to look at film stars, to see that all the money in the world does not make them happy. There is a price to pay for fame and fortune; they are always aspiring to perfection of the outer self, ignoring the disharmonies within. But if we were all connected to our real selves and that of our truth, our lives would not depend on the material trappings of winning the lottery.

We are all tired of working hard in order to make ends meet. There is an old saying that we do not miss what we have never had, but if we had them and lost them, how would we cope? The thing with life is that no matter what happens to us, good or bad, we do in fact cope, we may not like it, but we do cope, we get through it by becoming a stronger, and a much more balanced and resilient person. But once connected to our truth, good fortune would come our way naturally, where we would enjoy the things that we desired, connected to our truth, giving us abundance in all that we do.

Dreams only come true when we are really ready for them to do so, and they will not come true if our reason for wanting them is not about our truth, because we'll continue to block our efforts. Our dreams are about our higher consciousness and that of our higher self, reawakening us to our dreams that we promised we would achieve long ago, and are part of the life that was intended. Until then, we must continue to understand what our lives are all about, and to overcome the challenges that then bring the rewards beyond our wildest dreams or imagination. To be truly living our dreams is just an extension of who we really are, and once we've completed the journey, and embraced our creativeness of the real us will express its self in all that we then do. This enables us to live our lives to the full, expressing our natural talents, skills and abilities, and the uniqueness of these gifts that is our magical self.

So let's say for example we had accessed our highest self, and our higher consciousness, how would our lives change? Our lives would appear the same only we would view our lives from a privileged position of renewed clarity, clear vision and that of commitment to our true-selves and that of our dreams. We will feel supreme in our stature, our vibration feeling lighter and more vibrant, with us being more alive, and with a greater vision to look at life positively. We will achieve a knowing of what actions to take, staying focused on the outcome and then being accepting of what does or doesn't materialise. Everything around us is as it should be, to allow our truth to influence, and to portray our inner peace. Every aspect of our lives unfolding in divine timing, but more importantly, in the way that we pre-agreed it to be, with us feeling whole for the first time, in a very long time.

We must not feel threatened in anyway, to the outward influences or pressures of life that we may find ourselves under. Being light hearted, and also in helping others who are not as fortunate as us, with the giving and receiving of abundance, within every aspect of our lives. It's the realisation that our dreams are just that our dreams, we should live then for ourselves, and not be put off by others, who may feel threatened to the decisions that we've made. Because if we are our truth and others will be accepting of our decisions, being happy that we are able to live our life as it was intended for us all. Our higher vibration of the higher consciousness will lift the vibrations of those people who are close to us, and the benefits for all, is being able to achieve all that we desire.

Our dreams are our higher consciousness talking to our physical and mental self, inspiring us when we are in a relaxed state. But to give us the thoughts and feelings of our intuition, allowing us the opportunity to act on the instructions given. This creates the conditions or circumstances, which will allow the challenges to present themselves, giving us the opportunity to fulfil our limitless potential at all times. We then reawaken to our dreams, reawakening our memories of all lifetimes, of our natural talents, skills and abilities. So to accomplish all that we have ever aspired too, we must successfully eliminate the negative traits of our past lives, and the negativities of this lifetime. This enables us to understand our valuable learning's. So we can reawaken our dreams from long ago, by being able to access the Akasha records, and Esoteric knowledge, where all of our dreams, and the positive attributes of our achievements, and accomplishments have been recorded and stored for prosperity, since time began.

It is important that we enjoy the journey of the Souls Quest; it's a journey of infinite knowledge and wisdom, which we'll take with us from lifetime to lifetime, to enjoy and help us achieve our dreams and goals. We will accomplish the souls desire to live our life effortlessly, and within the divine order of the universe, and our creator.

CHAPTER 6

THE KNOWLEDGE AND WISDOM

The Knowledge and Wisdom is infinite, there is no new knowledge or wisdom it just evolves with us through time, from generation to generation, and all lifetimes. Our perception of that Knowledge changes as we understand our life's purpose in any chosen lifetime, and how we put the information received into practice, denotes our understanding of that knowledge, helping us to evolve to the higher levels of consciousness. Our knowledge and wisdom, is recorded in the infinite energy of the universe, which sustains all of creation since time began. The understanding of that knowledge is only accessible in our level of conscious awareness at any one time. As we travel through the different lifetimes, our level of consciousness evolves with us, and allows a greater understanding to life's purpose.

During each incarnate life our level of consciousness varies, depending on the pre-agreed soul's purpose, and the uniqueness of our potential, allowing us to achieve all that we desire to the best of our abilities, and to the good of mankind. The agreed level of conscious awareness that we will have at our disposal, and to use within this chosen lifetime, depends on what we have already understood and overcome, in order to understand the conditions or circumstances that we'd pre-agreed too. The agreement to all of the different aspects of our lessons that we need in order to overcome our valuable learning's of this lifetime, and were part of what we'd not fully understood maybe centuries before.

The level of our awareness will depend on the level of consciousness that we have already attained through the different incarnate lifetimes. The level varies depending on our circumstances and understanding of the truth to any given situation, and to the way we'd perceived them. The truth is about our inner selves, and to what we have come to understand within this incarnation. Because deep within us, is the truth about who we really are, and to what we have to overcome or accomplish, in order to evolve to the higher vibrational levels of awareness.

Throughout any lifetime we'll have created emotional imbalances that will cause us to stray from the source of the universal energy's that brings about the disconnectedness of our true selves. Our energy levels then become depleted, blocking the body's own natural energies, and that of the universal energy that enables our natural healing, these energies sustains a healthy existence whilst here on the earth plane. As we learn our lessons we gain greater understanding to our purpose, allowing our level of consciousness to evolve, which helps us recognise what is expected from us, during this lifetime.

The knowledge and wisdom, will aid us with the reconnection to our higher consciousness, and that of the higher self. As we evolve through the different stages of our lives, we will climb the conscious ladder of the infinite knowledge and wisdom, to reconnect with the divine energy of our soul. Gaining the knowledge, but on the deeper levels of consciousness, where we can attain the ultimate wisdom. When our earthly life is over, we will have achieved our goals that would help us to leave this lifetime, with our level of consciousness being higher than when we came into this life, hence, the purpose to our lives.

Our understanding of that knowledge will help us to continue our soul's journey in travelling through each incarnate lifetime, whilst searching for the answers that would transform our lives. The experiences of living our life, gaining the knowledge, and wisdom, to share with everyone we meet. All it takes to access this knowledge is the commitment to seeking our truth. The truth that would set us free from the restraints and restrictions that we have placed upon ourselves and others. Our perception to the knowledge gained will be received by our own level of understanding into the insights of awareness that we had attained at the time. The levels change as our creative awareness grows; we become open to the different ways of perceiving the information received. It's important that we are non-judgemental, but show compassion, and understanding, to ourselves and that of others. This leads to a deeper understanding of that knowledge, and the infinite wisdom then follows. Once we understand the uniqueness of this valuable insight, we can then access the information about our unique selves that has been recorded for prosperity.

We have all at some time or other, known the truth about something that has deeply affected us, but not known how or why, that belief is so strong that we have acted upon it, changing our lives forever. We all experience knowing thoughts this being our sub-conscious, our inner self, and the truth of our intuitiveness guiding us, and enabling us to make the right decisions. Once we have accessed the esoteric knowledge, it covers all aspects of our existences, giving us the truth of all that we need to know. When this occurs, we would truly achieve enlightenment, but if that's not to be the case within this lifetime, we would certainly achieve an enlightened soul status. This status would still be the ultimate state of awareness that we had achieved to date, and would then allows us to continue our soul's journey, of re-gathering all that we need in pursing the truth.

Knowledge and wisdom help us to appreciate all things in life, but more importantly how to appreciate our own lives first. Knowledge is an individual understands of the information received, and how to perceive it. The things that have happen to us or how we are actually feeling at that particular time will denote how we'd received the information given. Also to be taken into consideration is our awareness, outlook, and experiences in life to date, as well as our emotional states, because this will make a huge difference to how we actually perceive the different situations or circumstances around, and within us.

It is human nature to look at situations firstly from our own point of view, maybe judging others when we're not really in a position to make judgments. We can only look at any given situation using our past experiences as a guideline; so therefore, we could only ever see the problems from our point of view. So we must take an inner journey to reconnect with our true self, enabling us to recognise the truth of any given situation. Only upon doing so, would we then be in a unique position to see the other person's point of view, and to be able to offer an opinion that would be of any help. Because on accessing our truth, it would also access the insights which would then give us the greater knowledge of all that had passed and, the meanings to all of our experiences of this life, and other lifetimes too. This would give us a greater understanding, allowing us to recognise that how we had perceived what's happened to us, and making a judgment with only a small proportion of our truth, in other words with only a limited amount of understanding. Until then, our truth of all that had happened to us, had been hidden from us, hence the lesson. This would give us the wisdom to help us accept what's happened to us, and to help others also, in achieving great things for us all.

When I was going through my inner journey of the self, and to reconnect with my truth, I soon realised that how I'd perceived the different situations, had firstly been from my own point of view, with me not having taken into consideration everyone else's. With us all playing the parts that we were meant to play, in order for not only me to learn from but them too. Each and every-one of us was in fact playing out our own levels of personal truth, being influenced by our hidden agendas the only way that we knew how too, before being enlightened. No one is wrong in what they do, we are only perceived that way by us or others. This is because, none of us was actually aware of the truth that was hidden deep within us at that particular time, the truth about our existence and life's purpose.

The universal belief is that every one of us is just a small fragmentation of our true-self. With the real ascended us, guiding us through the different incarnate lifetimes in order to fulfil our soul's quest of experiencing a higher conscious life. We are all born into this life to travel the universe, before finding the secrets to life that's hidden deep within us, which would connects us fully to our truth, true selves, and would make us feel whole and complete once more. To be able to fully understand the significance of these important insights, there are a few unspoken laws to help us; we must never judge, and to be accepting of all situations, and to only see the good in everyone and everything. It's to be kind and tolerant of others, and to show compassion which gives us understanding.

When we accept that everyone is being their own level of truth, albeit only to their level of understanding at that particular time, and that no one is wrong in what they do, as we only perceive each other to be wrong because we all do things differently. But remember, we all do this in order for us to learn from, this is why we create the illusions within our lives in order to help us justify our actions. The understanding of this then gives us the greater knowledge, allowing us to view any situation through eyes of love, light and compassion, and being able to look at a much bigger picture of life in general.

I had recognised the part I had played within the production of my life; I could then see the parts that others also played in the production of my life, but more importantly their own lives too. We then realise in an instance that the things we thought were bad experiences, turn out to be wow! Actually we get this over whelming feeling that everything for the first time, in a very long time, is in fact fantastic. We did not get it wrong as we had perceived, but actually we'd made the right decisions and choices. We realise that we carried out our pre-agreement as was intended, and we actually feel excited with the prospects that what had happened to us was meant to happen, because we had learned our lessons, and most of all had survived to become a much stronger and confident

65

person with all aspects of our lives making perfect sense. Our actions and interactions with others, was as intended in the divine plan of our life in order to learn from, the understanding give us the greater knowledge, but more importantly access to the infinite wisdom.

So what do we do with this extraordinary insight? Every time we understand the different aspects of our learning's, our awareness and consciousness grows. Giving us more insight into the situations, and circumstances that we have to overcome, and that of learning our life's lessons. Our vision starts to become clearer, but if our vision lapse then our understandings may become clouded again, this is when frustration can set in because as with any new knowledge, we have to work at achieving it, in order to maintain a continuance of growth. The knowledge expands with our newfound level of awareness, and we will always be searching for more and more knowledge; it's our wisdom of that knowledge, and how we act upon it, and the vibration of that understanding will then be recorded in the infinite energy of all that is stored for prosperity. The more our minds expands, the more knowledge we can attain, this cycle evolves with us, and through time and eternity.

The more knowledge and wisdom we expose ourselves too, the greater the understanding, eventually allowing us to access the deeper levels of our personal understanding of our unique records, to the infinite mysteries of the universe, and beyond. This is the knowledge and wisdom, derived from our pure state of consciousness, since time began, and through the ages of time will have been written and rewritten, with our perceptions of that knowledge expanding.

The way we perceive that knowledge will alter our state of conscious awareness, and how it influences us, but also we then perceive our lives more positively. Only through the trials and tribulations, and the understandings of our lives, are we then able to even come close to the infinite knowledge and wisdom that would set us free. But this is the purpose of life;

66

it's all about the journey of self-discovery and reconnection of our authentic selves. When we have fully connected with the pure consciousness of our being and authentic self, our personal level of truth is accessible to us, stored within the Akasha Records, and Esoteric Knowledge, from when time began.

Once we have opened up to the infinite knowledge, and have successfully completed the reconnection of our true-selves, will we feel powerful, realising that we can manifest all that we desire, and that we'll be able to pursue our dreams with a clear vision of the desired outcome that we're aiming to achieve. To be knowledgeable is in the understanding of the truth about every aspect of our lives, but also about the situations or circumstances, and to how wee perceived the different events that have been played out within our lives. Once we can step outside of our comfort zones, we will realise the illusions that we'd created for ourselves, were in order for us to feel safe and secure.

When we have reconnected to our truth, it naturally opens us up to the greater knowledge that's within. This gives us a new lease of life, and more energy because we'll have connected to the power of our life force energy. This enables us through our higher vibrational consciousness to access the information that we'll need on a physical, mental and spiritual level in order to become successful. When we allow the mind to be uncluttered, giving us a clearer insight into what is real, and to what our lives have been all about, allowing us to access all the information when it's needed, to enable our continued journey of the soul's quest.

To be given all of the infinite knowledge and wisdom would be too powerful for us to cope with. The energy or vibration of the infinite knowledge and wisdom would create within us a form of madness, because our vibrations are not able to vibrate fast enough, in order to accommodate or cope with the entirety of the information or knowledge given. To be exposed to too much knowledge would give us sense of bliss,

67

as in the same state as raising our kundalini energy, the evolutionary energy of all knowing, a total state of bliss, that would leave us in a heightened state of awareness for hours or even days.

The knowledge that comes with the kundalini energy is very powerful, and an individual's innate power of divinity that is located at the base of the spine in a reservoir. The kundalini energy lies dormant within our bodies; it stays that way until we have understood our soul's journey. The inner journey of the true self and that of our infinite truth, and once we have successfully released all of our negative blockages from within, and reinstated harmony and balance, within all levels of our being. Only then could we consciously start with the preparation of releasing the kundalini energy from within, but to be able to release it naturally as this is the only way that this energy should be released. Word of caution! Never force the kundalini energy until you are ready to cope with it! Because once released, there is no going back. Forced kundalini can create illness, distress and disharmonious unrest of the soul. It should always be released under the guidance of a qualified kundalini teacher.

An enlightened soul of the kundalini energy would not find it easy to live within today's society. Our energies becoming so refined that we would need to retreat as we would find it difficult to do just menial tasks, retreating until we're able to handle this incredible phenomena. We would experience an instant knowing of awareness, also genius abilities, artistic, and creative skills, and we would have great powers of understanding, with us activating our supernatural gifts, such as levitation, astral travel and manifestation. We would also be a Supreme Being whilst here on the earth plane, achieving a connection with our ascended self.

Very few people actually achieve this state, but if we did, we would be all forgiving, all accepting, all knowing, and we would have unconditional love for all. We would have healing powers allowing us to heal all of creation; in fact we would be

68

fearless, being honest and trustworthy, and we will achieve all that we desire naturally and much more than our wildest dreams could ever imagine. So the kundalini energy is not only the evolutionary energy of all things, but the infinite knowledge and wisdom achieving total bliss. We would be at one with our-self and be in the presence of God.

We must all expose ourselves to our own personal truth, and then to expose ourselves naturally to the universal truth of the collective energy all that is. To become enlightened means to know the truth of the self, and how to successfully operate within the structure of our world, enlightenment is to be all knowing of the infinite knowledge and wisdom of all creation. This connection is the truth of mankind, and the only way that we can all sustain a healthy existence whilst here on the earth plane.

We are recycled souls, all in search of our infinite knowledge which would access the infinite wisdom of all times, allowing us to apply that knowledge into every aspect of our being and our everyday lives. This would ensure the continuance of life on earth as we know it, but in peace and harmony, in unity within accordance to the universal laws. This then gives us a wealth of knowledge, and the courage to tread within the realms of the unknown, but more importantly to be able to take back the control of our own personal power of eternal love, light and truth.

When we look back in history to the time of the Egyptians, they had incredible unexplained powers, and abilities. But more than anything else, extraordinary skills and insights, a knowledge and wisdom that was exceptionable even in today's standards. It does make you stop and think, how did they know, what they knew? How did they achieve what they achieved? Maybe it was just the fact that they were highly evolved human beings with incredible powers, and connected with the higher consciousness of the universal energy of all that is. When we're able to become at one with the powers of the universe, and with nature, we can then use our gifts, skills and abilities, to the highest good of all.

We all need to respect, and to understand the importance of living the life, that was intended by our creator, because the infinite knowledge is out there and within us, for us all to tap into the collective consciousness of the universe. To respect and honour the hidden secrets, and codes of ethics that will release all that we need to live abundantly within our chosen lifestyle. This creates a wealth of stability for us all, to form the foundations on which to build our lives upon, with a strong connection to mother earth, the universe, and the power of our creator. This is the source of universal energies, and the cosmic rays of eternal bliss of oneness, and by being at one with all that is, once more, allows us to be All Knowing!

CHAPTER 7

UNIVERSAL LAWS

The unspoken Universal Laws, what are they and what do they mean? Universal laws are about the natural laws of mankind, and how we interact with the universe and beyond, interconnecting as a whole, with harmony and balance between all things, unity of oneness with all creation. These laws establish certain actions, giving guidelines into the philosophy of life, a binding force that demands loyalty, honour, and respect.

The universe is a life force of infinite energy; it registers codes of conducts and ethics. So whatever we've done or achieved, the information is recorded for prosperity. The information is stored within the collective energy of mankind, it's a massive memory of energy that never forgets, and evolves with us through eternity. We can access the collective knowledge and wisdom anytime, in order to help us solve the mysteries into our existence, and in helping us to learn and overcome our lessons. It allows us to achieve our limitless potential of all lifetimes, to use to the greater good of everyone, and everything, in order for us to become our truth once more, and to attain the higher consciousness of all that is.

The power behind these universal laws help us maintain rightful action and intent, and with our thoughts and feelings, being pure in the knowledge of our truth, and helps us to know what the truth is of any situation. These laws have codes of conduct and ethics, and if practiced everyday enables us to live the life that was intended by our creator.

The laws give us access to inner peace that would enable us all one day to achieve world peace by each individual achieving their own peace first. To eradicate the

71

strife and suffering that's affected our world, and that of everyone, world suffering derives from fear, greed, and the power of control, and so on. The universal laws give us balance to know right from wrong. It allows us the conviction to know what is real from the fears of not knowing what's real, the illusions of the truth. By understanding and to worship the wonders of our creation would leave us in a powerful position. The power of the enlightened state that comes from the belief in our own unique abilities, giving freedom of choice to attain the knowledge that leads to the wisdom of living a life successfully.

The universal laws are infinite; they evolve through time, never changing. Our perception of these laws, changes with our experiences of life, with us not realising their importance. The laws of the land are written and rewritten through the ages, but with every publication we lose sight of their importance and meaning. If we search within our souls and reconnect to our truth, we'll find we have all that we need a true record of our personal achievements of all times. The positive skills and abilities, a wealth of knowledge that's held within the Akasha records, and is connected too and provided by the universe and cosmic energies, sustaining all of creation since time began.

The Universal Law of the Manifestation of the Lower Conscious Self

It's about honouring all aspect of the lower self, to respect our physical being and to maintain a balance between all things, which allows us to become Self-Aware. We need to recognise and act on the intuitive responses to all of our needs, with our intuition guiding us forwards. We need to witness our lives first and foremost, and have the ability to take responsibility for our actions and outcomes, readjusting if things are not as we hoped or wanted. To understand the importance that we do have a choice in the things we've agreed to do.

The Universal Law of Acceptance

When we accept all that happens to us, it's in order to become our truth, and accepting us with all our imperfections, we no longer beat ourselves up, thinking we've got things wrong, when in fact we've got them right. Everything we do, is what we have pre-agreed to do, so by accepting all that happens, is to give gratitude for the opportunities of the learning our lessons.

The Universal Law of Faith

To have faith in ourselves and faith in knowing that all that we need will be provided for. We have to have faith in God our life force energy, faith in others, and also faith in us that we'll succeed in fulfilling our dreams, and to have faith that all will turn out as it was intended. We need faith in our inner guidance, faith in religion, and our concepts, and beliefs in all things. But most of all we need faith in the Universe in its entirety.

The Universal Law of Forgiveness

The law of forgiveness is to be able to forgive ourselves, but also that of others. When we accept that everyone is right in what they do, we'll have less to forgive ourselves for. It's only the perceptions of what we do that denotes whether we or someone else, is considered to be wrong. None of us are wrong in what we do, as we're all living out our own personal levels of our truth. To forgive us is the greatest gift we can give ourselves because it will set us free.

The Universal Law of Respect

We need to respect all things within Gods creation, and respect ourselves, by respect us, others will respect us too. We also have to respect all of the universal laws, for they are very powerful, and also to respect our life force energy, nature, and every living thing upon the earth. To be respectful means not to be judgemental of others or us, but to respect their wishes, and to consider right action for all.

The Universal Law of Belief

Once we start believing in our true selves, we then start to believe in others, and the different situations or circumstances. To be able to believe in ourselves, we must recognise that everything we have done to date, we were meant to do. We must believe in the process of our lives, and recognise that everything happens for a reason, will leads to believe totally in us, nature, the universe, and in God the life force energy. Once we have belief in us, the world's our oyster; and we can achieve all that we desire, achieving our dreams, ambitions, and most of all, and our belief in all that's true.

The Universal Law of Living

It was Gods intention for us to live abundantly within our chosen life style. The law of living is that we carry out our promise, to live our lives to the best of our abilities, to be aware that we can provide for all of our needs, with the help of the universal laws. By not doing so, we will create the imbalances and disharmony within, because we have strayed from the source of the universal energy. By reconnecting with that infinite energy, we will start the process of living our lives by becoming our truth.

The Universal Law of Trust

We must trust in ourselves to fulfil our obligation to us, and then our trust in others will follow. We must trust that we will have good health, and our body's will self heal. To trust others is to be in anticipation, not being sure of the outcome, to trust in the self is to know that things will happen, and trusting in a positive outcome, when it's right for them to do so. Trusting in our personal truth, we'll have a clear vision of our goals, ambitions and dreams.

The Universal Law of Truth

We have an obligation to ourselves to become our truth, and to speak our truth, hear our truth, but also to see our truth. Our truth is all around us, every day in every way; our truth is deep within us. But depending on our circumstances, or the situations the lack of truth creates imbalances and disharmony within. Our ability to truthfully recognise, and understand the opportunity's that life presents to us, in order to reconnect with our truth. The truth of our life's purpose and learning's, and the truth about our actions and interactions, will allow us to be truthful about our thoughts and feelings. The reasons behind what we do are our truth, and the truth of our inner self, and higher conscious self, holds the secrets and the mystery of our incarnate soul.

The Universal Law of Honour

To honour ourselves in every way, to honour our word or action is to be honourable. We have to honour our queen and country, and all of creation, to honour our oath, and our responsibilities, adherence to what we think are right. When we fight for our queen and country or work for an employer, we have to be honourable to our code of ethics, what is morally right, so whatever we have agreed to do, we should carry it out to the last detail. We need to honour our beliefs, concepts, convictions, and to honour all of our promises. If we no longer enjoy what we do, don't justify it by blaming others or the situations, be honourable and admit defeat, and then move on.

The Universal Law of Peace

To be at peace with ourselves, then we are at one with us. We will then radiate peace to others, feeling calm, and relaxed. World peace is unity of mankind, so by achieving the universal laws gives us individual peace, and then eventually world peace. Peace is freedom from the restrictions and restraints that we placed upon us and others. Once we've released the disharmony and imbalances from within, we can achieve peace. To achieve peace is everyone's responsibility to themselves, but also in helping others to attain it for themselves also. From peaceful situations comes the ability to restore harmony and balance within our lives.

The Universal Law of Love

We need to love ourselves unconditionally, because until we love us, no one else can, this allows us to reconnect with our inner self, with us loving ourselves with all our imperfections. When we love us, we then say no to the demands of others, but to have compassion and understanding will allow us to know when to help, and how to help them. Love as no hidden agenda!

This completes the manifestation of the lower conscious self. In ACCEPTENCE of all things, we will have FAITH to fulfil our dreams and goals. We need FORGIVENESS of all things to heal ourselves, and when we have BELIEF in ourselves, all that we need comes to us. We need to show RESPECT in all aspects of our lives, and to be LIVING our lives to the full. We must TRUST our instincts and act upon them, in order to become our TRUTH, which allows us to HONOUR our word, deed and actions, in order to find an inner PEACE. When we LOVE ourselves we become happy and joyful. This is the completion of the manifestation of the lower physical self, allowing us to cross the bridge to the higher self, and that of our higher consciousness. With access our natural gifts, skills, and abilities enables us to manifest our dreams effortlessly, and helps us achieve our full potential to becoming our true-selves and that of our truth.

The Universal Law of the Manifestation of the Higher Conscious Self

It's about honouring all aspects of the higher conscious self, to perfect joyfulness, blissfulness and serenity, and to be in perfect harmony with life, the universe, nature and our true self. To allow everything to become into one, and the unity of our infinite power, which radiates from within, a beacon of divine light, energy and love. This gives us a strong connection to the abundance of the universal and cosmic rays, and a constant supply of the vibrational energies of our Creation.

The Universal Law of Abundance

To have abundance in every aspect of our lives, for what we truly need, the universe provides. We can manifest our desires, dreams and ambitions as good fortune comes our way, and we become lucky, finding ourselves in the right place at the right time. We begin to really live our lives to the full, as was intended by the universe and our creator, knowing abundance on a soul level.

The Universal Law of Supply

To receive everything that sustains a healthy existence on our planet, and being a part of the whole of creation. To access our Esoteric and Akasha records, and to be infinitely connected to the life force energy, enabling us to continue the cycle of our lives in achieving eternal bliss, maintaining a healthy mind, body and spirit, with realignment of our true-self.

The Universal Law of Equality

To be equal to all things, to know we are no more or no less than anyone or anything else. We are equal to our inner self and other half, and in perfect harmony with feminine and masculine energy. We are not positive or negative, but have a balance between all things giving us a serenity and poise.

The Universal Law of Mastery

To have mastery of our-self, and to have conquered all, being who we truly are, and life is our passion, with us being fully connected with every aspect of our lives and all things. To be connected to the family of life, in order to perfect our dreams, and to be successful in all that we do, allowing us to be our limitless potential of all lives.

The Universal Law of Oneness

All being, and to be at one with the whole of creation, to know Enlightenment, Pure Consciousness, and a journey of One Back to One, feeling complete and whole once more. We will experience an eternal bliss, and the coming together of all that is, in unity and harmony.

The Universal Law of Unity

The law of unity is the interconnecting of all things, and feeling whole once more, and to be a part of everything and everyone, interaction with all aspects of our creation. To be understanding of the infinite connection of humankind, and of the infinite energy of nature, but most of all, everything we need is deep within us. We are reconnected to the vibrations of the eternal and infinite energy of our world, the universe, and cosmic realms. We will have unity with the collective consciousness of humankind, our world, and beyond.

The Universal Law of Unconditional Love

It's about a love of all things, unconditionally with no price tag, without expectation of any reward. Unconditional Love is a connection of all things; it's the ultimate vibration of unity within our life force. It is the infinite love that supports all life, with us being naturally accepting. It's to love, no matter what? Our feelings and love never alters; we never feel challenged by others insecurities or decisions, being there for them no matter what. A powerful love that's unspoken, but the recipient never questions it. Unconditional love is the level of love attained from an enlightened state.

Once we have connected to all of the universal laws, they will lead us through life effortlessly; all we have to do is to respect them, to know their importance. This allows us, to become who we really are, our true self, our higher conscious self, pure light and energy of the divine and universal vibrations, being supported by our life force energy of the creator. To claim back the knowledge of these unique laws, will leave us in awe of the simplicities of the codes of rightful intention, and to be in a privileged position of giving to others less fortunate than ourselves, but to give unconditionally.

We have to rejoice in the opportunities, that we've been given, but to recognise that we have to give to us first, in order to truly be able to give to others. The laws state, that all we need is provided for, all we have to do is to go within and reconnect with it. Our life's path will have us travelling the universe to conquer and restore all that we need, in order to live a healthy and happy existence. The wisdom comes from knowing the truth of all that is from all life's experiences.

These universal laws are the secrets that delude us all, they are the answers to the questions, but more importantly they are our other half, they make us whole and complete, on all levels of our being and existence. Enlightenment is the reconnection with all of the universal laws, to be at one with the whole of creation.

So with the understanding that comes with the reconnection with our true selves, our higher self and higher consciousness is in the greater understanding of the universal laws. If we follow these laws they will enhance our lives, in accordance to the infinite power of enlightenment, and to be fully aware of the importance that all we need is provided by the universe.

All we have to do is to tap into the infinite energy and knowledge that will then raise our vibrations to a level of Awareness that brings together all that we need to access the true vibration of our existence, within the intricate workings of our unique world. The mystical wonders of creation, and to live a life worthy of living, free from the restraints and restrictions, from the unhappiness and strife that we had created for us.

It was not Gods intention for us to suffer; we have allowed us to suffer out miss-trust of our outmoded concepts, belief's and programming of how we perceived our world to be, instead of accepting of our world as it is. When we know the difference we can then change us within our world, from environmental issues to the ozone layer, and to become more spiritually aware. This process will allow us to raise our vibrations and become a part of the divine and universal plan, and to know that any positive action will make an overall difference to our planet and the self. The continuance of the soul's quest of achieving all that we desire in truth, light and love. When we live in accordance of the Universal Laws, we will achieve Peace and Harmony, and be in total Unity of humankind.

CHAPTER 8

THE CHAKRA, AURA AND ENERGIES

It is important for us all to become more body aware with the realignment of the mind, body and soul, which enhances well being. Our physical bodies are supported by our charka system, and an aura of vibrational energy that pulsates around our bodies, and we need to understand their importance to our existence, as they promote health. The chakra's unique action allows us release any negativity, and with their interaction with our organs, maintains health, by them being purified and cleansed by the continuous flow of universal, and earth's energy. When we understand the intricate workings of our chakra's and aura, and their relationship between our physical, mental, and spiritual being, we'll gain the unique understanding of how our bodies work within the structure of our world, and how everything is interconnected.

Each chakra has a relationship with the corresponding organs, but their main purpose is to keep us connected with the life force energy of the universe, which aids our physical bodies to be cleansed and purified, with the constant flow of universal and earth's energies. The continuous flow of energy cleanses the organs and provides Well Being for our entire physical body; all organs can be greatly influenced by the negative traits of our emotions, with our positive mindsets working to eradicate any imbalance. Throughout our lives we will develop weak areas where the mind will obligingly store the negative undertones of our perceptions. In some of us, these negative vibrations are already stored within our systems, just waiting to affect us when we have sufficiently exhausted ourselves with the constant battles from within. When we are ready to give up the fight of our outer pursuits, and surrender to the evitable pressure that we've placed ourselves under, life will intervene, giving us the opportunity to understand more about how our bodies work in harmony, and unity within the universal energy that pulsates throughout our unique energy system. As these energy systems become blocked, we begin to experience all kinds of ailments and discomforts. But with divine intervention and self-help, we can slowly begin to unclog these centres, so that we can once again maintain a healthy mind, body and soul.

So firstly what is a chakra? It is an energy centre; we have seven main energy centres within the body. These energy centres are fed directly from the universal energy through the top of the head (crown), going down through each energy centre of the body, cleansing and energising the body's natural energy system, and all organs, leaving the last centre at the base, which connects us to mother earth, where the negativities are neutralized. This is a constant process, the energy rotating through and around the physical body.

The first energy centre being the Base chakra is located at the pubic bone area. The second is the sacral chakra, located at the navel area. The third is the Solar Plexus chakra, located just below breastbone area. The fourth is the Heart chakra, located at the heart. The fifth is the Throat chakra, located at the throat. The sixth is the Brow chakra, located at the brow. The seventh being the Crown chakra located on top of the head.

These chakras are like a vortex that goes through the body from front to back. They energize the body's natural energy system, but over a period of time they may become blocked through negativity or misguided perceptions of our lives. The chakra's then become sluggish, to the point where they can become totally blocked, this creates the disharmony and imbalances within, often leaving our energy system depleted. When the disharmony is left untreated we begin the process of manifesting the discomforts, which leads to aliments, illness and eventually disease. When this starts to happen, our bodies will cry out for help in a number of different ways, hoping we'll take notice and do something to alleviate the imbalances.

When we fail to take notice of these discomforts, life then intervenes and gives us outward signals of what is going on inside of our physical bodies. Our body's defence systems then start to break down and our immunity becomes threatened. We need our chakras to be fully open so that they can draw on the universal energy that sustains our bodies, the energy that connects us to the life force energy. This helps us to achieve balance within, but also maintains the balance externally. It is important to achieve a state of balance on the inside, so we can alleviate the negativity that creates disharmony, because what's on the inside will be reflected on the outside of us.

When our body's natural energy system becomes blocked from the inside, no matter what work we did outwardly to counteract, it could never filter through to benefit us on the inside, and have a long term affect. That is why, whatever we've achieved on the outside of us, is only ever recognised for a short duration, in other words, we have the wow factor for just that period of time, and then it's forgotten. We often become distracted from our inner needs, with us telling ourselves we're ok when in fact we're not. Any work that we do on the inside of us, like self-healing, would have a positive effect on our well being and personal achievements, leaving us feeling good and contented, giving us a sense of oneness.

With the understanding or realisation of our needs, and the journey of our soul quest, will allow us to realise our potential and to live healthy within our chosen lifestyle. Whatever is within radiates outwards, and influences our thoughts, actions and interactions with others, as well as our relationship with all things. Once we have successfully cleansed, purified and opened these chakras fully, we can then start to feel energised, radiant and healthy.

The Aura is the energy system around the outside of our physical body; it has seven layers that protect the body. Their main function is to maintain a constant flow of energy around the body, free flowing energy, which interacts with the seven chakras. This gives us a constant flow of energy within and around the physical body, maintaining balance, harmony, reconnecting us to the universal energy and keeping us grounded to Mother Nature, and the earth's energy.

As we get problems within our bodies, these energy centres become blocked, and the energy within the aura becomes sluggish, with grey areas which represent blockages, negativity or illness. The energy can become so depleted that the person's appearance looks dull, they begin to look and feel unwell. So how we feel on the inside is now a reflection of the outside, we lose our radiance, we start to look older than our years, life's stresses beginning to take their toll. Because we are not made aware of this unique energy within and around our bodies, we can take it all for granted. Often waiting until the illness or disease has been diagnosed, before we take notice, or even action. By then we are so out of touch with the mind, body and soul, that we look to medical diagnosis and treatment to help improve our situations. It is not just about the physical body but the mind and soul as well.

So by understanding why these things happen to us, enables us to look at the possible reasons as to why it as happened. It's much more than what we've eaten or about what we've done or even about what we're not doing. But if were to take responsibility for our demise we could do a lot more, in helping ourselves. Remember conventional ways just treat the body; we need to treat the mind and soul likewise. Maybe one answer is in seeking some form of counselling or advice to help us understand the underline cause, helping us to change our lifestyles or even that of our mind set. This can be achieved in a lot of different ways, the understanding of how these energies and their collective qualities work in harmony with the mind, body, and soul.

By ensuring a constant flow of energy within, and around the physical body, we maintain health on every level of our being. Once we have understood the importance of the seven energy centres of the chakra's, and the different layers of the aura, we can then go on to understand about the next seven energy centres, and layers of our aura's. This understanding would help us to overcome, and achieve all of that we desire, giving us a stronger connection to the universe, and gain great insights into our uniqueness. The more chakra centres, and aura layers that we can activate and clear, the higher our vibrations will vibrate, activating our personal power of intention.

When we access our unique power of awareness, we are more attuned to the vibrations within and around us, with our physical bodies naturally releasing our gifts and abilities that enable us to be fully in our lives. These natural gifts and abilities, will help us to become more attuned to our body's many needs which enable our healing, and allow us to overcome the lessons as part of our life's process. Once we have successfully accomplished this unique technique of self-awareness and healing, we can activate the positive vibrations from previous lifetimes, giving us more knowledge and wisdom that enables us to achieve our limitless potential in all that we do.

The universal energy is the energy that sustains all of creation, and we connect with this beam of energy through the Crown chakra, and continue throughout our entire body, connecting with the Brow chakra, and Throat chakra, and the Heart chakra, then the Solar Plexus chakra, and the Sacral chakra and then finally the Base Chakra. The universal energy then connects us directly with mother earth, flowing upwards again through the layers of our Aura to reconnect with the universe, and then repeating the whole process continuously.

The universal energy gives us a constant flow throughout our bodies that rotates pulsating in energy, and completing the cycle in helping us purify, cleanse, and re-energise the body's natural defence mechanism, filtering throughout each layer of the aura, achieving balance and harmony. This allows the body's own natural healing abilities to do their work, in maintaining a healthy mind, body, and soul, with us bringing the different layers of the Aura, the Physical, Etheric, Emotional, Mental, Astral, Celestial and Ketheric bodies into realignment. This enables the manifestation of the higher consciousness, and the benefits of accessing the higher conscious level, is about accessing the higher self, reconnecting us to our true self, giving us the vital information of the knowledge and wisdom of our being.

The lower consciousness is that of our physical body, from the base chakra up to the heart chakra. Once we have cleared the negative blockages from these lower chakras, we can start the process of the reconnection to the inner self, where we cross the bridge from the lower consciousness, to the higher consciousness. The higher consciousness is from the higher heart chakra, up to the crown chakra and beyond. Connecting us to the divine knowledge and wisdom, and the infinite energy of the universe, the Esoteric knowledge, and the Akasha records of all that is, and this is our infinite wisdom.

To become aware of our chakra's we must be able to meditate, so we can go within to connect with them, enabling us to visualise each chakra in turn. We must free these chakras from any blockages or negativity, allowing each chakra to open fully. Once they are all fully open, positive energy can flow throughout the body purifying and cleansing, with the universal and earth's energies. This energy then interacts with the different organs within the body, to maintain Well Being, and this energy will sustain us all throughout our lifetime. When in mediation sit quietly with your eyes closed in a relaxed state where you will not be disturbed, then allow yourself to visualise each chakra's energy centre.

This is an illustration of the chakra system, and to how they function with their vortex's drawing energy from the earth and universal energies, aiding us in achieving well being.

THE SEVEN MAIN CHAKRA'S

CHAKRA SYSTEM

side view

UNIVERSAL ENERGY

CROWN — PURPLE

BROW — INDIGO

THROAT — BLUE

HEART — GREEN/PINK

SOLAR PLEXUS — YELLOW

SACRAL — ORANGE

BASE — RED

crown

base

EARTHS ENERGY

energy intake

the energy stimulates and purifies the bodies own energy field.

87

The first chakra is the base chakra, it's associated with the colour red, so when visualising this centre allowing it to become fully open with the colour red flowing throughout. Releasing the negativity or blockages, stimulating, purifying and cleansing this chakra, till you can see it glowing, this centre is connected to adrenal glands, kidneys and spinal column. The base chakra is connected to Mother Earth and keeps us grounded at all times.

The second chakra is the sacral chakra, it's associated with the colour orange, so as with the base visualise this centre releasing the negativity or blockages. Stimulating, purifying and cleansing with the colour orange flowing throughout this chakra, making sure this centre is also glowing and energised. This centre is connected to the organs of the reproductive system.

The third chakra being the solar plexus, it's associated with the colour yellow, so again stimulate, purify and cleanse, taking the colour yellow throughout the chakra, releasing the negativity or blockages, allowing this centre to glow. This centre is connected to the stomach, liver, gall bladder, pancreas and the nervous system.

The fourth chakra being the heart, its associated with the colours green and pink, so again stimulate, purifying and cleanse, releasing the negativity and the blockages. Taking the colours green and pink throughout the chakra, until the centre glows, this centre is connected to thymus, heart, blood and circulatory system. The reason this centre is associated with the two colours is because the heart chakra has a dual purpose, the green for lower heart chakra, and the pink for the higher heart chakra.

The fifth chakra is the throat chakra, and its associated with the colour blue, so again stimulate, purifying and cleanse, releasing the negativity or blockages, then taking the colour blue throughout the chakra allowing this centre to glow. This centre is connected with the thyroid, bronchial and the lungs.

The sixth chakra being the brow, it's associated with the colour indigo, so again stimulate, purifying and cleanse, releasing the negativity and the blockages. Taking the colour indigo throughout the chakra, allowing this centre to glow and become fully open, this centre is connected with pituitary, lower brain, eyes, nose and nervous system.

The seventh chakra being the crown, its associated with the colour purple, so again stimulate, purifying and cleanse, releasing the negativity and the blockages. Taking the colour purple throughout the centre until it glows, this centre is connected to the pineal and upper brain. The crown chakra connects us to the Divine and Universal energies, and other higher chakra's, and is important to our soul's continuance.

I have drawn an illustration on the next page of the physical body, and the different layers of the aura which is constantly fed by the earth's and universal energies, purifying and cleansing making our aura's radiate with vibrant energy in order to maintain well being.

THE SEVEN LAYERS OF THE AURA

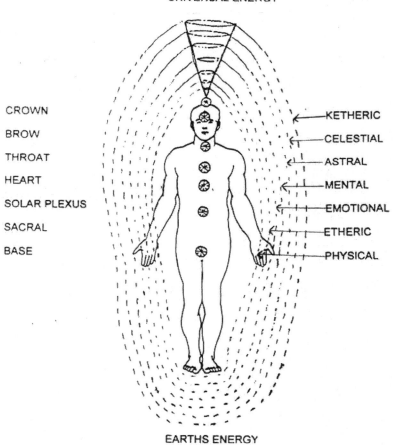

UNIVERSAL ENERGY

CROWN

BROW

THROAT

HEART

SOLAR PLEXUS

SACRAL

BASE

KETHERIC

CELESTIAL

ASTRAL

MENTAL

EMOTIONAL

ETHERIC

PHYSICAL

EARTHS ENERGY

layers of the aura in association with the chakra system.

90

The Aura can be cleansed again through mediation, just simply allow the energy within the chakra system to gently flow outwards through the vortexes into the different layers of the aura. Stimulating, purifying and cleansing, releasing the blockages or negativity, visualising the aura expanding. Your aura will pulsate with vibrant energy, watch the colours of the rainbow and also their pastel shades filter throughout the aura, just allowing the colours go where they are needed. After this exercise you feel more alive, with your energy vibrating and pulsating with renewed vitality, making you feel radiant. You will begin to understand your body's needs, by becoming aware when the chakras or aura become blocked. You will instantly realise when you need to cleanse the body, maybe just having to focus on one chakra, or just one layer of the aura. It's about understanding the relationship between each chakra, and their relative organs, and layers of the aura.

We take negativity on-board all the time, and depending on the nature of our problems, will denote where we actually store the negativity within our physical bodies or mind. If we are able to understand our life's lessons, we will then be able to release all negativity successfully. When we hold onto the negatives will only cause disharmony, and the different imbalances within. Creating ailments, illness, and diseases, but more importantly will denote our demise in death.

The way these negative trait affects our bodies, will depend on the nature of the imbalance, and with what has created our problems in the first place. Throughout our lives we will experience the different aliments and illness's, paying no particular attention as to why we are unwell. Not realising that our energy system has become depleted, making us more vulnerable to infections. The reason we catch illnesses etc is because we are not paying attention to our body's many needs.

The negative effects of illness's or ailments, and even that of disease will in fact tell us a lot about what is going on within our physical bodies, and the emotional or mental issues within. Maybe with us just suffering from a mental or even a physical fatigue, caused by too much going on at one time within our lives, and with us not being able to cope or find a solution to our problem. The imbalances or disharmony within our soul will tell us a lot about our past lives, and to what's happened to us, good or bad.

How often have we had a short break from our everyday lives, only to find ourselves ill? What happens is that we become so bogged down with the pressures of life that we do not have the time to actually listen to our body's needs. So when they do break down, it's much more than just rest that we need. If we only gave ourselves the same time, and consideration that we give to our best friends, or even to our loved ones, we would not become ill. The physical body cries out with an emotional need, an emotion that has been wrongly perceived, so stays as a negative trait stored somewhere within the body or mind, becoming a part of our learning's. If the emotion was due to our perception of being hurt by someone's actions or even of someone not acting the way that we wanted then too, then this creates a disharmonious imbalance within.

When we wrongly perceive the emotions out of an inward need that we have, and because we do not know any better, we look to someone else at times to fulfil those needs. When we begin to understand that it is only ourselves that can successfully nurture us and fulfil our true needs, we'll then be in a position to recognise the imbalances, so that we can understand their meanings and alleviate our pain.

Once we have achieved this we can become more truthful about what we really want or what is missing within our lives. It's not about the decisions that we make or even about the decisions that we in fact, do not make. It's about the way we allowed those decisions to affect us when the desired outcome did not materialise in the way we hoped for. By being accepting of all situations, we would not take the negatives on-board, and struggle with the consequence of any situation we found us in. Otherwise this will result in the negativity being stored within the appropriate organ, allowing the negativity to manifest, until the time becomes right, for us to do something about it. We go through life experiencing different scenario's, gaining a wealth of information, not realising that when the time becomes right, we can successfully put that information into good use, and action. This is our knowledge and it's to be used for the highest good of everyone concerned, allowing us to heal our lives consciously.

When we are able to tune into our body's many needs, makes us more aware of the real us, and our unique qualities. To release the negativity on a regular basis, helps maintain a healthy mind, body and soul. By being aware of the different techniques available to us will allow us to experience some of the well-kept secrets to the continuance of health, wealth, and happiness. Whatever our needs are, it's important that we take notice in learning our lessons that will help us restore health. The illnesses and ailment can turn into much more than just negative imbalances, making it a lot more difficult for us to cope with, let alone being able to comprehend the situation we then find us in.

Diseases can become very consuming; it takes all our efforts, and that of everyone around us, in helping us achieve a positive outcome. By dealing with these problems before they become out of hand, is all it takes to get our lives back on track, when we read the signs that the body's own defence system sends out to us on a regular basis, we can then stop these diseases etc, by eradicating the confusion or anguish. The bottom line is that these diseases do happen, if not to us then to someone close within our families. But by being aware to the possibility of the fact that it can happen to us, and that we do have choice of how we perceive the different aspects of our lives. We can then take back control in accessing the power from within, into releasing these negatives before they have the chance to multiply into something much more serious. So with the chakra's, the aura, and the different source points within and around the body, we can create Well

93

Being this allows our infinite power within, to manifest abundance within every aspect of our lives.

These issues, lessons and a responsibility to the self, helps us to understand the reasons of our life's purpose, and denotes which illness, disease or disabilities, that we have already in place within our physical bodies in order to learn from. If this is the case, we will find that our chakra's, aura, and energy system is effected with the imbalances, waiting for the right time to present themselves to us. So depending on how we have perceived our lives, will greatly affect our energy system and the different organs. Within our auras will be the negative traits of our learning, so it will act as an attracter field, attracting our lessons to us in order for us to overcome them.

Once we have successfully understood our lessons, the negativity will disappear; this is why like attracts like, because whatever is within the chakra or the aura energy system, will affect our vibration, effecting the physical body, mind or soul. If we end up making life hard work for ourselves, we will begin to store these negativities, within the chakra system, which then affects the organs etc, filtering outwards into the aura. This goes on to affect our actions, and interaction within every aspect of our lives, right down to our perception of thoughts or feelings. In understanding the emotional insecurities, and to how they affect us on every level of our being, will help us to understand the bigger picture of our lives, and what we have control over. To understand the interaction between all levels of our minds, body, and soul will help us to maintain perfect balance and harmony, within every aspect of our lives.

The more evolved we are, the less our physical bodies will be effected, and because of our level of awareness, will enable us not to take on-board the negative vibrations. This process allows us to deal with the problems at a much higher state of consciousness. Cause and effect, is about the understanding of whatever we have exposed ourselves too, we must take responsibility for our actions, and the overall outcome. We do have choices, but by not realising that, we

94

end up beating ourselves up at every turn, only to find us blocked by the continuance of our learning's. We get very disheartened by our efforts, our emotions ruling supreme. We do not always appreciate the intricate workings of the higher consciousness, leading us through the difficult trials, and tribulations of life. We will all eventually have to sort our problems out, whether here on the earth plane or when we have returned to the source. But whatever the case, we need the understanding of all of our lessons, in order for us to start the process of the evolutionary journey of change, all over again. The challenges of life, helps us to achieve our limitless potential, and by us not recognising our purpose stops us from becoming our truth, and then we cannot accomplish our dreams.

We have all that we need within our own natural resources of self-preservation; we came into this lifetime with them already set in place. The uniqueness of our energy system, the source of vibration that holds the carbon print of our resources that we have available to us, enabling us to overcome any situation that we may find ourselves in. When we identify our needs we then recognise our true nature, which gives us peace, contentment, and unity with all creation, but more importantly, to access the power of the universe that lies within each and every-one of us, and our carbon footprint of our true-selves and destiny. Our higher consciousness is the carbon print of all that we've ever been and of whom, we are still to become. We are pure energy, and when our time is up on the earth plane, we will return to the source where we continue to be a part of the life force energy of our planet.

CHAPTER 9

PAST LIVES

Our past lifetimes play a big part in which we are, and they form part of our characters, and the person who we truly are. So how do we really know how to deal with the discovery of this phenomenon? Firstly, we allow our memories of some forgotten time to come to the surface, either in our dream states or when visiting a place for the first time that we've felt an affinity with or when we've been doing things that have come natural to us, like skills or abilities. Or maybe we've met people that we have an instant affinity with, and it feels like we've known them for years.

When I was a child of about ten years old, I loved to dance, closing my eyes as I glided around the room, feeling I'd been a dancer in another life. I didn't know about past lives then, but I just knew that I'd been a dancer in concert halls, and the memory felt very real. I saw myself dancing to the music, with me knowing the dance routine, and the feeling stayed with me for a very long time. Later in life I discovered through past life regression that I'd had a life in the early nineteen hundreds as a chorus girl working in music halls, and theatres.

I had other strong feelings of places, situations, people, and countries throughout my life, not understanding there true meanings at the time, but eventually realising that we only address issues from other past lifetimes, when the time becomes right for us to do so. We have all had past lives; it's just that some of us will not be privy to the information within this lifetime, because we may have chosen a life without the help of our spiritual gifts, and abilities or even to be aware that other lifetime existed. I had such a life back in fourteen hundreds, where I denied myself on every level, so the reason for past life memories are in order for us to have a deeper understanding of all lifetimes that will be beneficial to our enlightened state of awareness.

In previous lives we would have experienced all of life's different scenarios, all of us at some time or other, playing the different roles in life. In some lifetimes we may have been rich or poor, good or bad, healthy or with disabilities and diseases, with us living in different countries or vocations of skilled work, and maybe some of us living off the land. We will even have had positions of importance, maybe even enjoying great wealth, living like royalty; we will have been both male and female, and played the different roles of brother, sister, mother, father and so on. We will also have had role reversals, so what we do unto others, we will have done to us, good or bad, this is why we must never judge others because we honestly don't know what we've done, let alone others.

At the time of our death within any lifetime, the mindset we had at the moment of our death is the one we take with us onto the next level of existence. This is why on death our lives flash before us, not in order to put things right, but for us to understand the experiences of our lives, and then to receive the understanding of what our life's purpose was all about. So the next life we have, we'll stand more chance of getting it right, depending on the different situations or circumstances, and the choices we then make.

Within any lifetime that we choose to be reborn in, we'll have pre-chose our parents, and the situations and circumstances that will make a big difference to our lives in order for us to learn from. Before we come back into any lifetime a lot of things can happen to us, for a while we will return to our greater good, to the life force energy from where we originally came. If for example we were really ill when we passed, we would need time to recover, giving us the opportunity to understand that particular situation and it's learning's. If we'd died tragically, again we would need time to recover from the trauma, and then be given the opportunity to understand that particular situation. If we were murdered, once again the traumatic situation would have to be overcome and understood.

I cannot tell you why these traumatic situations happen to us or to people very close to us, because that information is only personally obtainable to each individual, but I will share my experiences with you, and try to help you understand your own life's experiences.

I would be influences by my past lifetime memories in my sleep and waking state, as they reminded me of events that happened long ago. I was also able to access these memories by past life regression, and the art of kinesiology, a therapy that tests a muscle response whilst working on a higher conscious level. The therapist holds your arm in order to test the response to questions or to the problems that we're experiencing, and using charts of information can help to decipher the hidden truth about us and our imbalances within.

My first past life regression took me to a lifetime in 1444AD. I was 31yrs of age and I was female, within this life I deprived myself on every level, I was incapable of taking control of my life, and always looking for others to provide for me, often feeling resentment that life should treat me so harshly. The fact is, whatever happened to me in that life I did to myself because of the lessons that I needed to learn, only I could provide for all of my emotional, material, and financial needs, and by reconnecting with my true self I would be able to do this, so I used kinesiology to release the past trauma of that lifetime whish then released me within this lifetime.

In the same life I regressed to the 1458AD, where I died at the age of 45yrs in a horse and carriage accident. The wheels of the carriage ran over the left side of my body, interestingly, because all the injuries that I received in that accident were in fact problems or weak spots, which I had within this lifetime. Muscular problems to the left side of my body, and also to the neck, and once I'd addressed that lifetime all of those problems to the left side of my body disappeared. I died because I was struggling with my life, and my persona sent out the vibration of defeat which resulted in me having an accident that cost me my life.

Within this lifetime I also struggled with my life which caused me to admit defeat, where I wanted out of this lifetime because of my unhappiness. At the time I was 45 years of age, but with divine intervention I was prevented from taking my own life, because I'd agreed to sort it out this time, which I did, and I can only say how thankful I am because I am much stronger and wiser. I was in awe of that particular situation and by the understanding my problems allowed me to overcome them and go on to help others who are also struggling with their lives.

I regressed to another past life, in 100,000BC in Atlantis I was 16 years old, and female. The problem that I had to address within that life was I felt unlovable; the reason behind this emotion was because of my position in society. I was prevented from marrying the person that I truly loved, and I ended up married to someone more suitable to my status. My mind set at that particular time, was how I can appreciate a relationship that brings me only despair, I was blocked at every turn, no one gave a damn about what I wanted. So when I died it was with that mindset, and the lesson was that if I'd truly loved myself, and been connected with my truth, I wouldn't have had a problem with the person who I married, because it would have been my destiny to marry him. My truth was he was the person who I'd pre-agreed to marry in that lifetime, in order to learn my lesson of self-love. Within this lifetime one of my lessons was to understand the importance of self-love. The learning was that only I could provide that love for myself, and to feel that love on every level of my being, but I had to reconnect with my true self in order to achieve that love.

I also addressed within this present lifetime, the time of my conception, where I was struggling with the thought of having to be reborn, to deal with situations that had caused me great pain in the past, and to go through similar situations within my pending life. On this occasion I was being made to come back into this lifetime in order, not only to help myself, but others. Because by not loving ourselves or understanding the true meaning of unconditional love, we'll create all sorts of painful problems for us; this subject is part of my life's purpose, helping others to reconnect with their inner truth, and then embrace the unconditional love within. Knowing that I'd been through some very painful experiences within this life, gave me compassion and the understanding to help others, but only now as I look back and see the bigger picture of what my life was all about, could I truly appreciate those valuable learning's.

I regressed to another past lifetime in 835AD; I was 24 years of age, and female. I had been murdered in order for someone else to live my life, basically stepping into my shoes to enjoy the fruits of my labour. In this lifetime, someone else did benefit from my hard work, basically stepping into my shoes, enjoying all that I'd worked hard for. This lifetime was too painful to address, and the therapist started with balancing the negative energies on all of my emotional levels, it was to establish a proper and efficient free flow of energy through all level of my being. What this actually achieved made a big difference to my acceptance of what had happened to me within this lifetime. It gave me the information as to why my life had taken the course of events that it had, with it making perfect sense. Because what happened to me within this lifetime, I had created for someone else in another lifetime. I then started to see the bigger picture of my life, what a relief, because instead of thinking I'd made the wrong decisions within this lifetime. I suddenly realised that all the people connected to me within this lifetime, had actually played out their rightful parts in the production of my life in order for me to learn from, and overcome my life's purpose and lessons.

Another lifetime I regressed to was in 1107AD, again female, but in this lifetime I had nursed my partner in death, which had left me with inner crying, and I had not dealt with the bereavement before I died, leaving me with a deep sadness. I addressed another life in 1537AD and female, my partner died with his head in my lap. I felt I could have done more in order to prolong his life, so again the inner crying was not dealt with in that lifetime either leaving me feeling grief and guilt. So in this lifetime with all the healing and self-help that I'd administered, helping myself and others, the lesson I learned was, that we can help each other, but it's each individuals own responsibility to help themselves, and to do what they have to do in order to live a long and healthy life. We all have a responsibility to us to stay healthy, happy and content within all aspects of our lives.

It's sad when we lose those that we loved dearly, but we owe it to ourselves to survive no matter what, and to give ourselves the chance to live our lives to the full, for all concerned. We do this by dealing with our emotions or problems successfully, and not create the pain that comes from the guilt or grief of not dealing with our negative situations properly. Inner crying is about denying us the positive effects of our strong emotional and instincts of feeling the pain that's within, in order to deal with the traumatic situations within our lives as they happen to us. We all need to go through the grieving process at sometime or other but we need to this in a positive mindset in order to survive.

My learning's allowed me the opportunity to move onto my greater good, helping me access my full potential, and life's purpose. I would just like to say that if you decide not go down this pathway of past lives, you will be given other ways of dealing with whatever your life's lessons demands from you, and people everyday deal with their situations in their own way, but when they're ready to do so. But rest assured that no harm will ever come to you because you have chosen to do so, we all have our own unique ways of dealing with our lessons as they present themselves to us. If we miss the opportunity to understand these lessons, it will be given to us again, another day, and in another way. We all cope eventually with what we are given, so I hope I've given you

102

food for thought, as mentioned in my inner journey chapter, I explained how kinesiology worked in helping me to achieve my journey to my inner self, but this is just one of the many methods that worked for me.

Past lives are they really important to our learning's? No they are not; the only real benefit is that of a personal nature. The more that we evolve and spiritually grow, the more intrigued we become of the unknown, so this is purely one's own personal choice. I can only say from my own personal experience, that I have found it to be most beneficial to my understanding of the paranormal. It has given me an insight that as left me in amazement as to how everything interconnects. But if we have no desire to know about past lifetimes we still process our learning's but with us using other natural methods albeit over a longer time scale.

All beings are interconnected along with our planet and everything within its structure. Everyone at some time or other realises how small our planet is, and to how significant we all are, with us hopefully making a big difference to our world. Whatever we do good or bad will have an impact on us all, because it's about the vibrational energy that we send out, and how we all influence that energy in so many different ways, but also that energy influences us too.

We are pure energy, a spiritual essence of our true vibration before we were born, a state we will return to again, after we die, and when we have achieved our soul's quest. We are only a small part of our real essence, when we arrive on the earth plane. We spiritually grow and evolve, so that when the time becomes ready for us to know more about the real us, all will be revealed. But again only with what we can cope with at that particular time, if we became too eager to seek the power and to know more than we should, it would cause us great pain or turmoil. To be able to access the truth of all that is, takes us lifetimes, so don't force it, as it will come naturally to us when we are ready for it to do so, until then we have lots to achieve and understand.

To gain all the knowledge and wisdom, and to know all the secrets of our existence, would make us a powerful being, too powerful to be able to evolve whilst here on the earth plane, that is why the information of past lives, the influences of past lives and the universal secrets are only given to us in small doses. No one person could ever know it all that's why it's important to share these valuable insights with each other. When I was experiencing my gifts and unique abilities, and my different paranormal gifts that the feelings were so awesome that they blew me away, leaving me in such an enlightened state that it would take me a long time to come down from the heightened state of awareness, even though I have never taken drugs, I should imagine it's the same state, you feel invincible.

The universal laws state that we have to respect all things, so by respecting the insights to the unknown no harm will come to us. The only harm is created by our own fears, fear is a strong emotion because if we give into our fears, we would not be able to see the illusions of being fearful, and the opposite to fear is fearless which means bravery. Past lives did not harm us before we were aware of them, they can only benefit us once we've learned more about them, but whichever way we perceive it to be, it could only cause us harm or concern, if we did not honour the magnificence of the extraordinary insight into the real us.

These insights into the real us, what are they? They are our negative traits, the lessons we must learn, but by realising that we have done something similar once before, we're then given the details of that lifetime which makes the understanding of that life, more profound. That is why we must not judge others, for we do not know what we have in fact done.

For every past lifetime we address, the positive attributes from that particular time comes into play within this lifetime, bringing alignment and atonement to the mind, body and soul. This creates an oneness within which brings us closer to the real us, where we begin to feel whole, as the missing pieces of our lives just falls into place. This gives our characters more depth, with us feeling more in control of our everyday lives, making us worldly wise. We are then in pursuit of our true-destiny, with us effortlessly going through life, but with a smile on our face. We have a knowing of the secrets to the hidden messages of mankind, with our past-lives just being another way to finding the truth, but once the journey is taken, the comfort from knowing that the soul does go on, brings us a wealth of eternal bliss and happiness.

Karmic debt is what we pay back for our just deeds, basically for the pain that we have caused to others and ourselves in previous lifetimes, maybe through negative emotions such as greed, envy, power, betrayal, rejection, anger, cruelty, rebellion, resentment, ruined, hostility, vengeful, hate and more. To pay back means we have to put things right, to address our negative traits, to understand the reasons, to forgive ourselves, but also to forgive others for the parts that we've played in any given situation.

As I said earlier the mirror images are about what we've done to others, but more importantly, what we've done to ourselves. Our truth is that we did what we were meant to do in order to learn from, so once recognised it becomes a valuable lesson for all, no more procrastination, we and only we can put our part right for ourselves, but by doing so the other person or persons concerned, will also benefit from our understanding, by being lifted by our vibration to the higher energies, and the healing vibrations of the universal laws.

Instant karma is once we have addressed these issues, and we lapse or remake the same mistakes, life will instantly smack us on the hand. In order for us to instantly realise our error, this then saves us from any hardship or pain of the outward lessons, allowing ourselves to readdress the situation, which will then give us an even deeper understanding to our lessons of this lifetime.

Karmic credit, well this is the one that makes all the difference, because we'll have achieved this on successfully understanding the purpose of life, and we have now become an enlightened soul because we have reconnected to our truth, the truth about ourselves but also the truth about our planet, and how everything works in unity. We will have understood the importance of the divine, and the universal energy's and also that of cosmic energy.

We will see our lives in a new perspective, and we'll see everything to the greatest good of all, and only see the good in everyone. We will attract the positive attributes of life, the mirror image of what's within us. Everything we need will then present its self to us, in the divine timing, where we can access our abundance in every area of our lives. We then become more content with less around us, which frees us to embrace our lives with happiness, and joyfulness. We then experience peace, serenity, tranquillity and unity within all aspects of our lives. This will leads us to enlightenment, and allows us to connect with the pure consciousness of humankind.

CHAPTER 10

MIRROR IMAGES

The mirror images of life once recognised and acted upon, will change the way we perceive our lives forever, we will enjoy the challenges that life presents every-day in every-way, allowing us the opportunity to seeing the bigger picture of life. Mirror images show us the disharmony and imbalances within; they give us the opportunity to understand the reasons behind the negativities within our lives. Just remember, there is no such thing as coincidences, everything happens for a reason. They happen to allow us the opportunity of learning the lessons that we have to overcome. These lessons are part of our life's path, and we have pre-agreed to learn from them within this lifetime, so we can evolve to better times. These lessons will allow us to grow in every-way, mentally, physically, and spiritually, the lessons once learnt, would set us free from the restraints and restrictions that we hold ourselves too.

The illusions that we've created for ourselves over the years, were in order for us to understand the precious insights of our learning's. We were also given the details of the different events, conditions, and circumstances that would happen to us, and of their learning's. The unique messages received, and once understood would enable us to recognise the mirror images, and to what they were telling us. These lessons will help us to release the imbalances from within our lives, leaving us in awe of the learning's, and to how everything within our lives is interconnected. We can then put our lives back on track, so we can continue on our life's path, and experience our purpose effortlessly. We can then access our limitless potential of all lifetimes, and to be living our lives successfully, and too how it was intended.

So how do they work? We are all given situations that perfectly match the lessons we need to learn from. These situations can involve people or places; in fact circumstances that can affect us outwardly to reflect our inner state. Our mirror lessons can present themselves to us in anyway, we just have to be open to recognising them. A mirror image is a reflection of what's wrong within our lives, and can be reflected within the different aspects of our lives as well as the appliances that we use, in order to function within our everyday life. For example our car, washing machine etc or even the things within our work place, in fact anything that can show us a mirror image of ourselves. So whatever it is that's were using at that time, will show us our lessons. Situations or circumstances that we find ourselves in, will perfectly match our imbalance or disharmony within. This will enable us to face the truth of our actions or feelings, and even our perception of the understanding of the truth behind the problems, illness, and diseases etc. that may be plaguing us at that particular time.

Maybe we're just blocking ourselves from moving forwards or we might be on the wrong pathway, not being aware of what's going on around or within us. With us not listening to our inner voice or maybe putting others before ourselves, when our need is greater. Sometimes, it's about something that we do not want to see or hear; maybe we just need to relax more or take more care of ourselves, and simply just go with the flow of life more. It's about giving to us in order for us to successfully understand life's intervention; we can only give to others when we have successfully given to ourselves first. This will allow our energy levels to be restored, so our health is not compromised in what we do.

We need to take more notice, and pay attention to what is really going on within our lives. We really do have a responsibility to us first and foremost, otherwise the only person that we are neglecting or ignoring, is us. It is so easy to focus on others, because this prevents us from having to focus on ourselves and our problems, maybe because their very painful to do so. We'll do what is necessary to maintain an outer show of confidence, maybe just saying we're ok, when in fact we are not. People pleasing is one of the most common faults we have, living to someone else's expectations or simply that of our own would put us under too much pressure. We all have preconceived ideas to how we think things should be within our lives, not realising that others also do, and this gives us a conflict of interests.

We are often given the mirror images of us, whatever is on the inside of us will automatically be reflected on the outside, normally that of our insecurities, and the different problems or ailments. These mirror images give us the opportunity to learn from our negative emotions, and when the lesson that we've attracted is played out; they become the learning's that we came into this lifetime to understand and overcome. So until then, what we show the world on the outside is not a true image of the real us on the inside, as we're not being our truth. It's just a reflection of us with all our imperfections, of which we are not comfortable with.

When we can successfully understand these mirror images, we then start to put things within our lives right. Once we put these mirror images into daily practice, we can then begin to understand the philosophy of life. We get instant recognition, and then our vibration lifts, giving us continued access to our higher consciousness, and to the knowledge and wisdom, which then attracts the positive mirror images of our lives. The positive mirror images will bring the opportunities we need in order to become successful in all that we do and desire. They will bring happiness, contentment, and restore health, even a sense of achievement, that enables us to activate our limitless potential. This allows us to live out the rest of our lives, living abundantly within our chosen lifestyle.

I will explain some of my mirror images to show you how they work, when something within our car brakes, and by discovering what the problem is, we can then use it as a mirror image for us. Just say the exhaust falls off our car, what can

109

this be telling us? Maybe we're exhausted and hadn't realised so, and by understanding what function an exhaust system has we can understand the mirror image? An exhaust gets rid of the fumes, maybe we're angry or even fuming, and we'd not recognised that fact. Or maybe we just needed to let off steam; also it maybe because we needed to understand what was within or even to just acknowledges that we're really angry at something or someone. If the disharmony within is left untreated, it will create an imbalance which eventually leads to negative weak area within the body, these imbalances eventually become illness, disease, or aches or pains and so on.

Maybe we've got a flat tyre, this could be mean we feel deflated or let down by someone, but the truth is, we are letting our-self down by not being our truth, and fulfilling our dreams or promises. By not recognising the disharmony within until now, our health maybe compromised somehow. Say our brakes have failed, and then maybe the mirror image is telling us that we're out of control and should slow down. Only the individual concerned, can work out their mirror image of what happens to them, get the picture?

If our car stalls, then we're stalling over something, and we need to make a decision. Let's just say we're travelling at high speed in the fast lane on the motorway, the person in front of us will not move over to let us pass. The mirror image here is about us and the other person. Firstly they are blocking someone or preventing someone from moving forwards, and we're blocking our-self and hadn't recognised it or maybe we are out of control, and need to slow down; this applies in the car, as well as within our personal life. So by looking at the mirror images every-day, with the items that we use on a regular basis, we can then try to understand life's messages.

When we do not take heed because we have not recognised the imbalance within, life intervenes giving us the opportunity as best as it can, in order for us to take notice. So now let's look at the mirror images with all of the people we meet, and those we spend our time with everyday. What we perceive are our learning's, and what others perceive are their learning's. Say someone is being awkward with us, the mirror image is, we are being awkward with ourselves. I have listed a few emotions, and their opposites below.

Their Action / Life's Action Your Interaction

Rejection	your Rejecting the self
Ignoring	your ignoring the self
Betrayal	you have betrayed yourself
Blaming	you are blaming yourself
Unlovable	you do not love yourself
Restrictions	you restrict you and your life
Denying	you are deny yourself
Fighting	you are procrastinating
Uncaring	you do not care for yourself
Disrespectful	you do not respect yourself

Now to look at these scenarios from their action, if someone rejects us they have also been rejected, maybe in this life or a past lifetime. They may have become fearful of that negative trait, because that's the lesson they too have to learn, by not rejecting themselves, so they will not be rejected, and then will not reject others or the different situations or circumstances within their life. When we understand the different scenarios in any given situation, it's important to remember not to do unto others that we would not have done to us. As we will discover when we begin to learn, and understand these lessons, what we did to others, whether in this lifetime or in other past lifetimes, we'll have role reversal in this one. So I will explain a few of my lessons of mirror images.

I was cheated out of my material, and financial wealth that I had worked hard for, and in a past life I had cheated someone out of their wealth. So hence the lesson! In this lifetime, I denied myself of what was rightfully mine; so basically, my persona had sent the vibration out, for me to be deceived. I was deceived, and even though it nearly destroyed me, I learned a very valuable lesson.

Also within this life I'd helped others to gain everything that I wanted for myself, denying myself on every level. In a previous lifetime, I denied myself on every level, which eventually ended with me losing my life, because I did not want the struggle with living any more. So my life was taken, and within this life, I came close to losing my life, but with divine intervention it was prevented from happening. Because I had pre-agreed to sort it all out in this lifetime, that was the lesson, not to deny myself on any level.

When we deceive others, we must each take the responsibility to learn from the situation, in order to put it right for us, and that of the other person or persons. When we have paid back our karmic debt, we can then accumulate karmic credit were we can enjoy the fruits of our labour, and not that of working hard just to maintain an outer show of success?

The only real wealth is that of honour and respect, and only we can provide for our needs, but more than anything else, to love ourselves because we would then realise we were worth so much more. All that we need to do in helping us to be successful in all aspects of our lives is to reconnect to our truth of all of our existences. Because in doing so, we get a greater understanding to the reasons behind our problems, which are not really problems, just life's obstacles that once accepted, can be overcome, and the learning's become part of our characters, and achievements. This gives us an inner strength, of knowledge and wisdom that is all a big parts of our makeup, of the real us.

So to look more closely at the mirror images, and understanding the lessons for ourselves, gives us the insight into what is happening not just to us, but others too. This gives us the compassion, and understanding that we need in order to not judge others, because we do not know what we've done in previous lifetimes, and I believe we have done it all, good and bad. We must find it within us to forgive others as well as ourselves for the parts we've all played within the production of our lives. We are all living out the different aspects and scenarios of our truth, and hidden agendas with us, hoping to become our truth of all lifetimes, but only when we have overcome, and understood our life's purpose and lessons within this one.

Every one of us as to learn their own unique lessons, even at times of total despair, these lessons can be very difficult to comprehend, and to know their true meaning. Their learning's will not just help us to understand and learn from, but they will help others to get it right in the future. I know that by being tolerant and kind, and in allowing others to excel in their own time and at their own pace, will give them the opportunity to learn their own valuable lessons, but when they need too.

If someone asks for our advice, we can only give it if we are detached from his or her problems, this allows us to be compassionate and understanding, by us being aware that whatever lessons they maybe learning at the time, could be very painful. Sometimes the learning's are very painful that it causes us to shut down, in order to protect ourselves from our emotional anguish.

I personally at times had done just that, by allowing myself to be effect by things that happened to me that were beyond my control or because of the pain that I'd created for me by thinking that I'd got it wrong, the pain was so over

113

whelming that I got discouraged. When this happens to us we often put the learning's off until another day or even telling ourselves we are okay, when we clearly are not. But the thing we must remember is, if that is the case, then do not procrastinate the self, because the truth is we are human, and sometimes even the most evolve person as times when they can't cope with life's trail's and tribulations.

The day that we do address our problems, is the day that we are meant too, so there can never be, what ifs or maybes! We spend far too much time beating ourselves up all because we feel that we'd made the wrong decision or mistake. The truth is it's only wrong if we do not learn from, and understand and overcome the situation, but again it's just another part of the learning's of life. No Pain, No Gain.

So just imagine all of the problems you've had in the past choose just one of them, and try to understand the lessons that you're meant to learn. Thinking of the mirror images that was present at the time, but you didn't realize the significance of them. First think about how you were feeling were you being truthful with yourself regarding the situation? Were your emotions playing a big part? Did you feel insecure, hurt or threatened in anyway? Did you feel out of control or were you struggling with life in general, and was feeling disappointed or was it about the pride and ego, because things were not going to plan? Maybe your life was not going the way you'd hoped for; the more you struggled with the lessons in life, the less that you understood what's expected of you. Feeling whatever you do will end in failure, and its human nature to hold onto what we can at times of traumatic situations.

We all allow the negative emotions to overawe us, maybe, because we feel needy or insecure, vulnerable or even experiencing emotions of anger or guilt, and we felt the situation was controlling us. But whatever the case, we could do nothing to change what had happened but it affected us greatly. When we have fully recovered we need to release the imbalances that had happened to us because life's traumatic situations can get locked into our mind, body and soul and need to be released before they caused harm.

The more we try to get things right, the further we push our dreams and ambitions away, falling into past mistakes again and again. Not realising that we do have choices, we often think that we are being punished in some way; we think life is so unfair, sometimes blaming others or even that of God for our hardship, thinking we are being punished in some way. Saying why has he or she let this happen, when in fact they did not, it was us all along, maybe self-sabotaging our own efforts. With us only making a light hearted attempt in getting it right or we may have hoped that someone else would take control, to sorting our problems out. Life sometimes wears us down, with the struggles becoming too much, and we think we are making progress only to discover we have failed again, or that we have not quite achieved the desired outcome.

Remember that everything that we perceive about our lives is an illusion, until we reconnect with our truth. So how we perceived the different situations, will tell us what is wrong within our lives at that particular time. Frustration plays a big part in what drives us on; thinking that this is not what I really wanted. But by going along with it, eventually you end up where you were meant to be, and we just needed to have more faith, even when we feel everybody has deserted us. We needed those experiences in order to overcome our obstacles, but we need to be able to view the different situations within our lives truthfully. When we become detached from the desired outcome, we stand more chance of getting it right, and achieving our goals. To see our truth, and to have belief, faith and trust in us, will allow us to be more accepting of the outcome.

When we are on the right pathway, life runs smoothly, and everything just drops into place, the right people, job, even the decisions we make will allow us to be successful. We never rejoice in our good fortune, because we take the good times for granted, but we allow us to be totally consumed by

115

our bad times. The mirror image of other people's down falls is that it has not happened to us, making us realise how fortunate we actually are.

They always say someone's loss is someone else's gain, this can be personally, emotionally, physically, even materially or financially, in fact in any situation we find us in. It's human nature to only focus on the things that we feel we haven't got within our lives. We forget to focus on what we do in fact have, often giving into our needs or wants. Our truth is to focus, and rejoice on all aspects of our lives every-day. We take life for granted and get complacent with us forgetting to cherish those we hold dear, our families and friends or our material, and financial wealth, the food on our tables, or even just to show gratitude for our health.

Our pride and ego creates a lot of the illusions within our lives, and without the mirror images to show us what's real, and to where we are going wrong, we wouldn't be able to understand the lessons, that we need to learn. The mirror images of life are there for everyone's benefit, it's not the other person's fault if they have learnt from their life's experiences, and you have not. Sometimes we are so close to the situation that we cannot see the wood for the trees. At those times we should take a step back, maybe using the other persons mirror lesson as our own learning's.

So it's about being truthful regarding to the outcome of any situation we've found our-self to be in. If we have any doubts within in our life, and you do not address the situation, we end up denying ourselves the opportunity to do the right thing for all concerned. It's never too late to put things right, because if we don't put it right in this lifetime, we will have to address it in another. Remember role reversal; do not do unto others that you wouldn't have done to you. The wrongs that we have done to us, by others, are a part of our lessons also, remember two wrongs do not make a right.

116

When we start to read our mirror images, it doesn't matter if at first we get it wrong, because we'll be given it again later, with us becoming more aware of what's going on. When we help others to see their mirror images, it will give us more understanding of our own mirror images. At times we are so close to our own problems, the answers or solutions just seen unobtainable, but by looking or focusing on other people's problems their solutions seen easy to work out. It's important to take onboard the learning's of others for ourselves because by doing so, it can make it easier for us to see where we are going wrong, and what it takes to put our lives right.

Communication is the greatest gift of all, because by being in the family of life, broadens our horizons, and helps us to be living in the now, making us realise how fortunate and privileged we really are. When living our lives in the present time, gives life the opportunity to present the many lessons we need, allowing us to enjoy many adventures. We meet lots of interesting people along the way, some of whom we were meant to meet, all being a part of the divine plan, and destiny playing its role within our lives. Others just making life more adventuresses and rewarding, because the more people we meet and who touch our lives, the more lives we can touch. Helping us all to get closer to the understanding of our personal truth and to the parts we're all playing in the divine plan of our lives.

The mirror images of the people who are closest to us are a fascinating subject to observe. These lessons can make or break us, maybe causing us great pain or grief. When two people come together, whether in marriage or just a relationship, and when they both meet for the first time, they'll both experience mirror images of the other. Opposites attract, so our weakness will be their strength, their weakness will be our strength, but within then both, will be the negative traits of each other, waiting for the right time for them to present themselves. This is why we are with all the people we hold dear, they're all part of the divine plan, the people that we need in our lives, in order to understand the different scenario's in the production of our life, and all lives.

We would all have been in various past lives situations together, playing the different roles but trying to understand the lessons. So if we accuse someone of not loving us the way that we want them to, its mirror image is that we do not love ourselves. If we accuse someone of neglecting us, we are in fact neglecting ourselves. Now if the other person accused us of not loving them, that's because they do not love themselves. If we do not love ourselves, then we are not in a position to feel that love or any love that was shown towards us, and we end up questioning that love.

So our loved ones are a big part of the divine plan, they are in our lives, as we are in theirs, to overcome similar situations. So we will live happily together, helping each other with the different aspects of our learning's, encouraging and being supportive. If we were more accepting of each other, we would not take what happens to us as a threat to our happiness, and to just accept that there is a problem that requires the two of them to overcome it. It's not necessarily any one's fault, hence the mirror image lesson, it's about give and take, and being there for each other no matter what. Once we successfully accomplish the lessons together, we can then go onto better things, and better times.

Throughout any relationship we will have periods of the ups and downs, but the longer we stay together, the more chance we have of eventually becoming soul mates. We do not start off with soul mate, only the potential of a soul mate, because if we successfully learn and grow together, they will perfectly match our ideal partner or mate, our mirror image of ourselves. We must value our loved ones they are precious, bringing laughter, and sunshine into our lives, and offer love, comfort, and support.

We have to be careful that we do not totally rely on our spouses or partners, and even that of loved ones. It's important that we take responsibility for ourselves, being separate but together. It's about being able to survive without the other if we had too. Because then we would all become self-sufficient, providing for our own needs, but also that of the others unconditionally. We are all individual, and we do things in our own time, hopefully being true to ourselves, and the person that we attracted as a partner in life is a lifelong partner but we don't always recognise it as so. Just know that we do not fall out of love, regardless of the love that we feel for them. It's just that we misplace that love, allowing our frustrations, fears, and emotions to create the illusion of unhappiness. When the traumatic time as healed, we will realise that the unhappiness was created out of the lack of love for ourselves that we'd wrongly perceived, and then justified our emotions by creating an imbalance or disharmony within the relationship, and with the self.

When we reconnect to the love that's within, we'll realise that true love was there all along, just waiting to be rekindled and nurtured, setting us all free. Love has no hidden agenda; it's given unconditionally to hold within the palm of your hand just like a butterfly, because if we hold it too tightly we will crush it. We need to give love it's freedom to come and go, and to have faith that in letting the things go that we cherish, we recognise how dear they are to us, and we never lose those that we truly love.

Unconditional love allows us our full potential to love on all levels of our being, because by not feeling threatened by the separation of our loved ones, but to allow the divine to do it's magic. We cannot lose love, we never could, we've just misplaced it for love is eternal, and so whether it's our own personal love or the love of another, even if we've lost someone in death or by a separation then our love for them will always be within our hearts and souls, for love in eternal. To connect with the real inner you, and our truth of all things, is solely to reconnect to the divine love, and Unconditional Love. This is the love that will set you free.

CHAPTER 11

DISABILITIES, DISEASE, & SYMPTOMS

We are all a product of what we do, say, feel, think and eat, its cause and effect of what we expose ourselves to, so what we give out, is what we get back. We are also greatly influenced by our past lives, as well as this one. Some people are born with disabilities, diseases, conditions or symptoms within, and a question that people often ask is why as this happened to me or even why is this happening to us or even how could God let this happen? Whatever happens to us, it's difficult to understand what it's all about. For some of us, these conditions will happen at sometime or other throughout our lives, and hopefully some of us escaping with just a few physical, mental or even emotional scars. So what is the answer?

This is not an easy subject to write about because of the people whose lives have already been greatly affected by such situations. If only we could be more accepting of our situations or circumstances, but at times it's difficult to comprehend, let alone understand. If we were our truth and connected to our true self, then our inner journey would enable us to accept all things that have happened to us, good or bad. Sometimes things are so tragic that we feel that we could never understand them, let alone overcome them, leaving us barely coping with the enormity of the consequences. Once we can accept these situations, and have made peace with others, ourselves, and God then the healing of the soul would take place. The healing on the outside will then automatically follow, allowing our body's natural healing abilities to work miracles, but we have to be connected with the divine and universal energies, so that the negative or emotional blocks or issues can be naturally released.

Our problems seem easier to bear once we have understood the reasons why these things have happened to us, in the first place. Then and only then, does life begin to make sense, and we are able to start the healing process that would enable healing throughout all of the different levels of our unique energy system, of our mind, body and soul, healing our lives. This will allow us to fulfil our dreams and we then stand more chance of getting our lives right.

The problems that we have with our health are being able to understand our physical bodies or that of our higher consciousness talking to us, and helping us to recognise that we have a problem that needs attention. When we are aware of the problem we must overcome the imbalances or disharmony within, which may have created the diseases or illness's, which has manifested by our emotional imbalances or negative belief's, maybe punishing the self in some-way. We have to overcome the important lessons that we must understand and learn from, and once accepted, we can start the process of releasing the emotions that has caused the illnesses etc in the first place. Sometimes our illnesses are caused on an emotional level, but at other times on physical or mental level as well. We must also learn of our past lifetime lessons; this will give us a greater learning on the deeper fundamental levels of our soul. As we continue to evolve, we achieve greater understandings, giving us the infinite Knowledge and Wisdom, of our greater good.

If we're born with these problems already in place, and we'd already agreed to them before we came into this lifetime, it's in order to obtain greater understanding of the lessons we must learn. So this chapter is about what we do to us through the errors of our learning's and to the cause and effects that have resulted in not overcoming them. We are a product of our own miss-understanding to the lessons or even to the possibility of our complete ignorance to the fact, that something might be wrong within us.

Right from birth we start to take on board emotional insecurities of the situations that we are exposed too, but also this happens as we start to look to others to meet our needs. As babies we need our parents to love and care for us, but as we become more independent, we start to develop our own characters. So depending on what we're exposed too, denote what happens to us and to how we perceive it. We are being programmed by others and society, having to meet their expectations as soon as we are born. Even what we watch on television or read in magazines, in fact anything that we expose ourselves to, will greatly influence each individual. We then aspire or become a product of our own expectations, but the secret in life is to make our own minds up to what we want or need from life. As a small child, we are made to do things that others consider to be beneficial to us, but in accepting those decisions, we can then learn from them, and then make our own minds up to what we want to do, later on in life.

We need to accept the good, with the bad, because if we don't accept the bad and learn from it, it will be given to us again and again, until we do learn, but if we chose to not learn it will eventually cause us great pain. Sometimes we can feel resentment of others who are controlling us, not realising that the negative traits of our persona, are in fact allowing them to control us. This will eventually cause disharmony and unrest that leads to ailments or illness, if left untreated. Remember that we all came into this lifetime to overcome issues, with the negative traits already in place; this is a part of our inherited characteristics and learning's. It would have been a lot easier if we had been born with a manual tucked beneath our arm, telling us what our lives would be all about. We sort of have a manual, only it's written in our palms.

The right palm is an actual record of what's happened to us in past lifetimes, recording the important information about our achievements, accomplishment, gifts and talents. Also our personal characteristics which will place us in a privileged position, once understood and acted upon. It also records our anguish and traumatic situations, with fate playing a big part leading us forwards in achieving our true-destiny.

The left hand is our potential, and what we can achieve once we have recognised the opportunities as they present themselves to us. So we do have the information about which we really are, and they are the details that tell us a lot about us, all we need to do is decipher the coded messages, and truth that's been hidden from us and a good palmist could do this for us. When having our palms read, be careful not to misinterpret the information given, out of desperation for details for the future, when we have not understood the past or even been able to live our lives in the present time, achieving all we can successfully. By accessing our higher consciousness, we can then access our hidden gifts, skills and abilities, and the secrets into our limitless potential, giving us back the control in our intended destiny, life, and that of our truth. For nobody can predict our futures better than us with commitment and self-effort, and us connected to our higher conscious self and truth.

So how does it all work? Different diseases, illness etc; are triggered by different negative emotions, and then our emotions are triggered by situations or circumstances that happen to us, within our lives. So depending on what has happened and to how we perceive the different situations, will establish how we then take the negativity on board. If we are fearful, hurt, or even disappointed by the outcome, our emotional state and sometimes the things that have happen are so subtle that we do not realise what has happened to us, until it's too late. Often telling ourselves that we are not bothered, when in fact we are, being told it's a weakness to cry or to be angry, and even to show what is considered any negative emotion. But the fact is, no emotion is negative, it is the natural body's defence system kicking in, to advise us of a problem or even to the dangers that may be present, and we need to be aware of in order for them to be dealt with.

124

By looking at the problems and then understanding the lessons, we will naturally deal with the situations, releasing the emotions, not allowing any harmful negative imbalance to lock into the subconscious. Babies naturally experience all of these emotions, but with love, trust and faith in their chosen parents they can deal successfully with their emotions, releasing them naturally, the positive attributes of instinctive behavioural reactions, to the negative issues. From an early age children become fearful of what they are exposed too, but also because they are sensitive to the natural instincts of the unknown, often becoming afraid because the fear of the unknown is usually passed on by members of their families, it's so easy to pass our fears onto those people close to us and especially if they are sensitive.

Fear is a destructive emotion because we can become fearful of life, which can influence all that we do in negative ways, self-sabotaging our efforts or putting obstacles in our own way. Fear is probably the most difficult emotion to overcome, the reason being that ninety-nine percent of the time; we put on a brave face, using the emotion of fear incorrectly, because fear is a positive emotion as it would leads us away from danger and not into it. Our fears can be very destructive creating irrational imbalances, causing us to be fearful of the unknown or even change. When our fear triggers emotions from long ago, it can bring illness and disease into our lives, manifesting from symptoms or conditions that we've already have within us just waiting to be activated by our fears.

The disabilities, diseases and illnesses, all start with conditions and symptoms, so at this stage we can do something about it. We do have choices, even though we may feel we don't, because of the outward influences. But the truth of the matter is, because we are not facing our truth; we can then be in denial, creating the illusions about what is really happening to us in our everyday lives. Let's look at disabilities, they can be a result of an accident or even an illness influenced by our perception, creating a mental disability that then becomes a physical one.

So why do they happen? Because we have not been paying attention to the finer details of life, maybe we've put ourselves in a situation where the inevitable happens. We all have a responsibility to ourselves, maybe by just accessing our higher consciousness; we would have heard that small inner voice that would have lead us away from danger. By not hearing our inner self, what's happened to us was part of our life's learning. There is a reason as to why, these things happen to us, even if it is hard to accept, because it's about the much bigger picture of our lives, the truth of who we really are. We are all influenced by the unseen forces of our learning's, having programs running that makes us a victim, until we have overcome the lesson. Clear vision, is in having faith in ourselves, a clear conviction of facing our truth head on, when we have successfully faced our truth, all will be revealed, when it's right to do so. No other person can tell us why it's happened to us; it is up to the individual to seek out that information for themselves, giving them greater understanding into their life, and how we are all interconnected.

So let me give you a few examples of past life traumas that have created this lifetimes disabilities and diseases, also the disharmony within. If in a past life you did not learn your lessons and had created ailments and illness's before you died, you would then be reborn into whichever lifetime you agreed to overcome those problems. To be given the lessons again, will help us recognise the significance to the understanding of the uniqueness of our own power of thought, and actions. In realising that we do have choices in life, enables us to make the right decisions resulting in good health. If we were born with a disability, it could derive from injury that we sustained in a past life, maybe resulting in our death, and we didn't have the opportunity to rectify the problem or learn the lesson. It could also have been about injury we created for ourselves or that of others, due to our

126

lack of respect or consideration for life in general, being given a taste of our own medicine.

You normally find that people born with disabilities are far more accepting of their demise than those who experience a disability during their lifetime. It could be that they pre-knew of their situation that enabled them to be more accepting of the disability. However the people who look after them, again their lesson will be in looking after a disabled person, maybe it's just a case of role reversal or the possibility of an injury that we may have inflicted on someone else in a past lifetime. By accessing the truth, all will be revealed; we will all know our own personal truth about the different situations within our lives, deep within our subconscious.

There is an old saying that we do not miss what we've never had, and disabilities can create a disability of the mind, because there are people who have achieved incredible things, with their disabilities not being a problem. We can achieve great things in accepting our demises and overcome the most awful situations or circumstances within our lives. These people become an inspiration to us all, showing tremendous courage and strength, but most of all, that the impossible can happen and that good does come from bad. By accepting all situations we can overcome anything, and this helps us with the transition of the lower conscious self to the higher conscious self where miracles do happen, and allow us to become our truth and power once more. Diseases can also derive from our miss-perception of situations or circumstances, which we were unable to fully understand, within this lifetime or a previous lifetime.

We all have emotional insecurities that we've brought with us into this lifetime, to be played out, once the time becomes right for them to do so. We must allow us the opportunity to learn our lessons before the disease or illness as the opportunity to become much more than a condition or symptom, allowing us to recover completely. The mind greatly influences the body, the aliments being part of the divine plan, in understanding how we are all a part of a much bigger picture that involves all of creation. In the understanding of what's required of us in order to reconnect with our life force, will show us how vulnerable we are, because we've strayed from the source.

The universe states that all we need in achieving Well Being will be provided for us, as long as we are aware of our dilemma. In recognising our imbalances and disharmony, we can then seek help, whether it's self-help or that of other's. In experiencing our own unique abilities and accessing our spiritual gifts, healing takes place, but we need to become our truth, to understand that only pure intention can create the miracles that we need to overcome the most difficult diseases, and illness's that plague us today.

Diseases such as cancer are about deep hurts, shocks to the body and the emotional effects of traumatic situations. Some say that cancer is within all of us, just waiting for that trigger that will set it off, but this is also true of any disease, we are at times born with conditions or symptoms, and the inherited negative traits with us, and this is why the same illness or diseases run in families.

We are all dealing with similar lessons to learn, remember this is why we chose our parents to learn from, we choose them and they chose their parents and so on. This is about the bigger picture that once recognised, will open us up to other similar characteristics within our families that play an important part into our life's production. How often have we heard someone say "I will not do as my parent's do," maybe just picking up on one of their negative traits. Interesting though, how we do not recognise their positive traits till later in life.

When we find ourselves doing exactly what are parents taught us to do, that is why we chose them as our parents, in order to learn both the positive and negative lessons, and learning from both parents is important. Our children chose us,

128

so if we learn our lessons before the time becomes right for them to face their lessons; they automatically receive the benefit of our labours. In the future they may be tested to see if they have continued to learn in order to pass this valuable information onto their own children. This is the only true legacy to give to our children and for them to pass onto their children, and so on; it's the knowledge and wisdom of the greater understanding of the family of life, and to the purpose of all life.

I have listed below the negative and the positive traits to some of the different diseases, illness's etc.

Ailments and their negative and positive thought process:

Alzheimer' is about not dealing with life, and to embrace life will help to release the negative thought process.

Arthritis is feeling unloved and so we must love ourselves with all our imperfections letting go of hurt or bitterness.

Back problems are about a lack of support, so to ask for support or to give you support will alleviate your aches and pains.

Cancer is about the inherited hurts or hurts that we've acuminated through life's experiences, so understanding and dissolving those hurts can heal cancer.

Constipation or Bowl problems are about holding onto the past and not living in the now, and allowing us to go with the flow of life.

Deafness can be about the refusal to hear, with us not listening to our needs and by not listening to our truth of all things.

Diabetes is about not living your life for you and denying you, we need to be true to us whilst living our lives for us.

Epilepsy is about rejecting life, to rejoice and engage our lives fully.

Eye problems are a refusal to see clearly, we need to see with love and joy.

Headaches are our mental controls of our life, let go of the controls.

Heart is about self-persecution, so to heal the heart requires self-forgiveness.

Infections are about anger or irritation, to be joyful and peaceful in all you do aids well being.

Kidney problems are about disappointment or criticism, to be accepting of all situations heals our lives.

Lungs the ability to accept and absorb life, I have balance and harmony within my life.

Muscles problems are the inability to move forwards with our lives, to move forwards with easy, joy and balance in perfect harmony.

Pain is about the guilt we feel, I am free to be me and I forgive.

Every ailment, illness, condition or disease as a negative emotion attached to it, and by altering our perception can alleviate these problems from within our mind, body or soul.

The above are just my interpretations of the negative emotions and their positive opposites; everyone is unique to themselves, so we will have our own interpretation of the aliments and problems, within our lives. All we need to do is to understand the workings of the part of the body that is affected, then using the mirror images to see what we are in fact not doing, whilst trying to maintain well being. For example say you have a problem with your stomach, the stomach is about nourishment, so you are not physically nourishing the self on all levels, so you need to see where you're ignoring the self. So by being open to the lateral way of thinking, it's the understanding of the emotional blackmail that we hold ourselves too.

The reasons behind our actions, because this theory of us doing things for others as an undertone of dishonesty, we all do things in order to make us feel better or doing the different things out of justification of our expectations or that of others. Maybe by focusing on others, enables us not to focus on what is really troubling us, we all revel at sometime or other in other people's dramas. This is because, we don't have to cope with our own pending drama, pretending everything is fine, when really it's not.

So remember the mirror images, like attracts like, life's intervention really does show us our own disharmonious situations, the disharmony that eventually leads to illness. We often allow ourselves to become depleted within our unique energy system, that our immune system weakens creating the different ailments, illness's etc; we really are a product of our own doing. Once when I was suffering from a viral infection, I realised it was the result of pushing myself too hard, helping others when my instincts had told me to rest, but because I did not want to let others down, I chose to ignore that small voice from within. We can only give to others when we really are in the position to do so. Everyone has a responsibility to himself or herself first, but we have conflicting emotional battles within, the natural instincts of self-justifying our decisions.

The theory is we do what we do, because it's required for us to learn from, so hence the lesson. In the actions or choice I made, I was invalidating myself, I had not thought I was good enough to put myself first, and on addressing the issue; I recovered within hours of going down with the virus. It's right that we help our fellow man, as required by the universal law of helping others less fortunate. But had I not ignored the problem within myself in the first place, I would not have

131

become ill, so therefore I wasn't in a position to give my time when I needed to look after me first. The undertones of our actions affects us greatly, not only by inflicting illness on ourselves, but consequently inflicted the viral infection on others.

The disharmony within makes us feel that something is missing within our lives. The thing missing is our truth; it's our own personal truth of our purpose, and intended life. The unrest created from the disconnection of our truth and personal power, creates the problems with our health, in accepting the lessons and not fighting against the self, we are able to re-educate the mind, body and soul in achieving a Well Being state. We can change the way our physical body feels about the illness or disharmonious situations, once we've realised what it is, that we're not doing. In most hospitals today we will find alternative remedies and techniques, running alongside the conventional ways, realising that there is more to illness than meets the eye, it's about treating the course of the illness, the emotional imbalances, but more importantly our mental perception to that illness etc.

Our medical or holistic practitioners experience incredible unexplained miracles within their profession, but sometimes they look for a scientific explanation. It's about healing the Mental (mind), Physical (body) and Spiritual (soul), in order to perform a miracle cure. To heal on all level is important to maintain Well Being, allowing us to become part of the universal energy that gives us a constant flow of energy between all levels of our existence. This process enables us to reach and realise our limitless potential. What is our potential? It's living our lives in truth, and with balance and harmony, with unity and peace restored as our creator intended but also to embrace our unique gifts, skills, and abilities. It's our miss-perception of unhappiness that creates our physical problems, we're all meant to live life to the full, but to live it in accordance of the universal laws.

There are a lot of self-help books on the market, which will help to re-establish a healthy mind, body and soul, all it takes is for us to understand the imbalances and disharmony within. Once we have accepted the part we've played, we'll then be able to reverse the command signals that the mind has sent out to the physical body. Our thoughts are very powerful, so if our beliefs of ourselves are negative, they'll cause the body to respond in a negative way. We can think ourselves into feeling ill, as well as feeling really good about ourselves. Our bodies respond to our pampering, it will also respond to neglect of the self. So what is life all about? It's about giving us the opportunity to undo all of our miss deeds from all lifetimes. Where the pain and grief that we've created through generations of miss-guided beliefs into thinking we're hard done too!

God really did not intend for us to live a life of emotional grief, created by thinking we are being punished in some way. God does not punish us; we punish ourselves, because we have forgotten to live in peace, harmony and in unity with mankind. We have forgotten to honour and respect, all of creation. But more importantly we have forgotten the promise we made to ourselves, before we came into this lifetime. The promise to learn our lessons gracefully and accepting the good times, as well as the bad, because they are all a very big part of the real us, and our learning's. Disabilities, disease, conditions, illness and ailments, are all a product of the emotional blackmail that we hold ourselves too. They are the negative traits of the imbalances and disharmonies within, filtering through the different levels of consciousness; once we understand these disharmonious situations they will set us free from the restraints and restrictions, and the beliefs of our old programs that control our everyday lives.

To experience a miracle in our evolutionary journey, from the physical level of consciousness to the spiritual level of our higher self, and that of the higher consciousness that would heal our lives. Exposing us to the vibrations where miracles do happen. First we must play our parts in allowing ourselves

133

exposure to these wonderful gifts, and allow us to gratefully receive the re-establishment of our uniqueness, of our true-self, and the gifts and abilities of all our past lifetimes, and beyond. Because once we've set our self-free from the controls of our everyday life, we'll experience Gods Will, to accomplish all that we desire, and live abundantly within our chosen lifestyle, but more importantly to be healthy, wealthy and wise.

CHAPTER 12

OUR PHYSICAL LIFE

We will have arrived within this lifetime, with the date and time of our birth being pre-arranged because of the positive effects of astrology, and the influences of our planetary, lunar and solar systems, and their effects on the human personality and behaviour. Also we would have pre-chosen our parents, because their weakness will be our strength, and our strengths will be their weakness. We would also have chosen the place where we would live, the people we would meet because of their influences being important to our learning's and life's purpose.

We would have pre-chosen our partners, siblings, religion, and also our talents, skills and abilities, some of which will not be evident, until the time becomes right for them to do so. We would also have pre-agreed the situations, conditions and circumstances of all the events within our lives, and their desired outcome. Our lifestyles and positions within society, in fact all of the experiences that are considered our fate, and part of our life's path. Even to the cause and effect of the different situations and circumstances within our lives, even to the way the physical body responds to the negativity will denote the outcome of our demise. All that we pre-agreed would perfectly match our pre-destined destiny, and even our death is timely with the way we die negotiable, because of our learning's and the understanding of those lessons.

When we are born into this chosen lifetime, and our memories of the agreement that we pre-agreed is wiped from our memory, in order for us to travel our life's journey in search of the truth of that agreement. Maybe, our memories of the events to happen are erased by the trauma of our birth? Everyone around us rejoices our arrival, at that moment we are pure, trusting and accepting of all of our emotions. We stay in a pure state of consciousness, and unconditional love until we are ready to start our learning journey, and start to develop our personality and characteristics, with us being influenced by everyone, and everything around us. So our journey as begun, from that moment on we start the process of elimination, even as a small child, our higher consciousness and that of the inner voice will be guiding us along the pathway. Remember the choices that others are making for us as well have our own, are also a big part of our lessons and the understanding of those lessons.

Our earliest memories of this lifetime are from about two years onwards, so whatever happens to us will denote what we in fact do remember later on in life. Our lessons can actually start from conception, birth and all through our years, to the moment we die and beyond. For some of us they will also include past lives, where the learning's can be quite profound. But whatever we do in fact remember, will play a big part in our understandings of the lessons, and to how we perceived the information given. The things that we do forget are the situations or circumstances that have caused us great pain, and we've stored within our sub-conscious, with us forgetting them until the time becomes right for us to face our truth about the learning's, and the reasons as to why they happened. When the time becomes right, all will be revealed, until then it's about self-preservation and survival.

We are all given situations throughout our lives where we have to cope, even with the most horrendous situations. They say that we are not given anything that we couldn't cope with. The reason we cope is because we have pre-agreed to those learning's. Because deep in our sub-conscious we know of the events that will happen to us, giving us an inner strength, that's why we do in fact cope. Sometimes we experience Deja vu, a memory triggered deep within our sub-conscious from long ago. By not being accepting of our situations or circumstances, we'll cause ourselves great pain from the lack of trust, faith and belief that all will be revealed in time.

We start our earthly life with our learning's already in place, and depending on what we do, and to how we perceive the different situations or conditions, will depend on how our bodies and minds respond to the understanding of those lessons. Some of us are a victim of our negative traits, and then they send signals to our minds, which then influence the physical body, and then our bodies start to take on board, and store the negativity, causing stress and tension, which if ignored, creates the disharmonious situations within. So as we walk our chosen pathway, we will be given the different situations to overcome, but we must bear in mind of the unseen force of our higher consciousness, which is driving us on to overcome the obstacles within our lives. With us knowing that we've placed them there, in order to experience as part of our learning of how we self-sabotage our efforts because of a lack of faith in us.

It is important that we take an active part in living our life. It's about being fully in our lives, and not just going through the process of life with no real effort. Maybe just putting up with what is going on, thinking that we have no control. So it is important that we learn the lessons, but to when we learn them, is entirely up to the individual. We must ensure that we do take responsibility for our actions and the outcomes. At no time are we made to do anything, which we didn't want to do, no one is making us do the things, which we in fact do, no one that is, except ourselves. We must bear in mind that everyone works to his or her own time scale and hidden agenda, but also to the different ways of doing, and to our perceptions and beliefs of the different situations.

We must be more accepting of who we truly are, and not trying to be who we are not, but also to be more accepting of us and others. There is a lot of controversy into what life is all about, and of the many things that are expected from us. It is our actions to ourselves, and the interactions with others, which denotes the understanding of our responsibility to the outcome, readjusting to things if they're not what we want. Due to fear we often just go along with the different situations, not really realising that we do have choices to make, and that the right choice will allow us to evolve to the higher vibrations. But more importantly to understand the motives behind our actions, for they will alter the desired outcome, giving us back, the control to our everyday lives.

But the most important thing about life is ourselves, because if we are not able to live our lives to the full, and to be able to activate our desires and ambitions to achieve our dreams, what would be the point to us being here? We're here to be given the many opportunities that we in fact do get, every day in every way, allows us to be fully in our lives, and to search for our truth of what our lives are all about. Because by reconnecting or accessing our truth, we would then be able to learn our lessons and grow spiritually, physically and mentally. The sooner we learn the less negative effect or harm, to our physical body, or our mental state, and then the perception of the understanding would influence us positively.

By accessing our truth, is just the first part of our own personal quest, because once we understand the bigger picture of our existence, the less we then rely on the things outside of our physical body. When we take more care of the inner us, this then helps us to get rid of all of the things that we no longer need or want. We then go through life with no excess baggage, freeing yourselves, in order to receive all that we desire, allowing our vibration to vibrate at a higher level, giving yourselves a much healthier approach to life, which gives us a healthier mind, body and soul.

The physical body is a representation of the real us, so whoever we are on the inside, is not necessarily who we show on the outside, that is until we have reconnected to our truth. Our truth being the real us, only our truth should radiate from within, affecting all that we do in a positive and beneficial way for all. So to reconnect is the journey of the one, back to the one, and if we decide not to reconnect while here on the earth plane, we will be given the opportunity to reconnect once we've returned to the spirit world, where we can understand our lessons. The lessons that would make a big difference, to the continuance of the soul's journey, becoming whole and being able to return back to the source. Sometime in the future we would again pre-agree another agreement to another lifetime, the circumstances and the situations being different. If we have not previously understood the lessons we could end up, reliving the same lessons all again.

The body is unique in the different ways it responds to the influences of our divine and universal energies, also to all life form, including nature, but most of all, to the unseen force our determination, the will and the unrest of the soul. The negative emotions are a product of our fears, shall I fail, will I be happy, or will I die before I have the chance to live abundantly? These emotions are part and parcel of our learning's, the negative traits are a product of our learning's, creating the disharmony, we are not able to see the way ahead. We may not even be able to find a solution to our endeavours. We beat ourselves up at every opportunity, because things are not going as we would've liked or hoped for. But we're not always aware of the procrastination, until we feel the unrest within that then demands attention to alleviate.

We all have our pride and ego sending out the vibration of defeat or even of being a victim to thank for our physical problems, ailments, illness or diseases. Even accidents which cause injury or disabilities are a part of the pride and ego. We take injustice to the control that we have placed upon ourselves, sometimes seeing it as others controlling us or even that of situations and circumstances. When the truth is, we're controlling situation etc in order to learn from, and others controlling their own set of situations. But that word acceptance says it all, to be accepting of all that's within our lives; we will be open to receive what we need, because by doing so, we'll only receive the positive learning's. By not doing so, we'll only receive the negative traits, and then the lessons will be given again. Albeit in different ways, but we'll be given it again, until we do understand the importance of its learning, this having its toll on the physical body.

All of our emotions are positive they are the strong feelings, which could lead us away from pain, danger or a situation that is not beneficial to our highest good. By ignoring or giving into these fearful emotions, only feeds the pride and ego. Our emotions are natural, so we should act upon them, and then release the emotions that have created our problems. To hold onto these emotions would be harmful and destructive to the physical body, creating the imbalances within. As with all of creation, the answers to our problems are all around us, everyday, in every-way. So whatever our beliefs or even to what our personal endeavours are, we should be able to find the right way of solving our problems, and to learning our valuable lessons.

Our inherited lessons or problems stem from either generation to generation or from past lives, along with the negative traits of our learning's during this lifetime. So remember all situations or circumstances happen to us for a reason, the physical body is just the vehicle that we use within any lifetime, even though our physical appearance changes, along with the different aspects of our characteristics. We are influenced by our past lives in all sort of different ways, so we must be careful that our learning's don't take their toll on the physical body. So by being aware of the problems within, we hold the power to rejuvenate, invigorate and to influence the body's physical being. We also hold the power of trust, faith, and belief in our own unique healing abilities, in being able to restore natural health, so by us listening to our bodies many needs, we can change the way our physical body feels and reacts, by embracing our higher conscious self of all our lifetimes.

Remember that all aliments are our body's own defence mechanism; it makes us aware of the disharmony within, created by the disharmonious situations. Sometimes we are unable to heal our lives, because we have disconnected from the energy within, once we have reconnected to the energy, healing can then take place, allowing us the opportunity to overcome our problems and to realise our vision of our intended life. Our perception of the situations within our everyday lives influences the energy field within and around our bodies; this then, infiltrates our physical being. Our perpetual state of altered awareness creates Well Being, our continued ignorance of our demise, will result in the various disharmonious situations within our physical bodies, which will then create the imbalances, within the mental and soul levels.

When we leave the earth to return back to the spirit world, we will leave behind the physical body, but we'll take with us the vibration of the physical, mental and emotional bodies, having reconnected to our collective consciousness and then we gain understanding of our lessons. We will then be able to let go of the negativity from that lifetime, and the essence of our truth will transform us back to light and love of our source from where we originally came. So in respecting the physical body as the shroud of the real us while here on the earth plane, would bring harmony and balance to every level of our being. Because without a healthy physical body, we could not live our lives as was intended.

We need to evolve successfully, so the soul essence can live on, to continue the soul's evolutionary journey, to better times, but more importantly to register the codes of mastery within our lives. The overall secret to life, is to not to buy into the negatives, and by not doing so, we will not to give our power away because we've been influenced by things that we have no control over. We then stay connected to the infinite power that sustains all growth, it's a power that is unique to us, and is fuelled by our own personal belief, faith, and trust in us and all we do. The truth of what is really going on within our lives, will allow us not to give our power or gifts, skills and abilities away, through lack of disbelief, faith and trust in the real us.

We are never really content, with the appearance of our physical bodies, maybe focusing on being too fat or too thin. We want long hair, when our hair is short; we want to be fit, when we are unfit, always looking at the opposites of what we have. We pay too much time and attention on perfection, maintaining an outer show. Sometimes pushing ourselves to the absolute limits, not realizing until we become ill that the disharmony within was created by not recognising our truth, and accepting our true selves with all our imperfections. We always try to aspire to standards or expectations of others, even of our own belief system, we only end up with creating a lot of unrest for ourselves, because we are not accepting of all that's within our lives, and not giving us a chance to be who we really are.

When we have successfully reconnected to our true selves and that of our energy within, we would firstly love ourselves on all levels of our being, and eventually unconditionally; we would then feel really comfortable in our own skins, loving ourselves no matter what. So whatever as happened to our physical bodies during our life, and if we have not left it too late, we would be able to reverse the conditions, illnesses and so on. If you have disabilities, you are healed on a soul level, where the physical body is not of so much importance; our life would not depend on perfection, because we'd be accepting of our truth. The real truth that would set us free from the restraints and restrictions that we'd placed so securely around and within our lives.

Our truth is who we really are, being the continuance of the soul, whether we're still here on the earth plane or even after we've departed from this life, because the truth of our soul is eternal. In an enlightened state of awareness, the physical body does not hold its position of priority into what we think is important any more. We will allow the real us to radiate from within, accepting of all our imperfections, which are as much a part of us, for they're our unique qualities of our true characters.

People aspire to people who can accept themselves for who they truly are. If we can laugh at us, we would know that we're really comfortable, with whom we truly are. The importance of the physical appearance of each and every-one of us, are the illusions that we show the world to hide our imperfections, not realising that these are in fact, our best attributes. Because they make us unique, they make us physically different from everyone else; they are a big part of our characteristics, the distinctive qualities that sets us aside from everyone else. Proving to us and that of everyone else that we've understood the importance of what we truly are, and that we've become accepting of all things within our lives. Having survived the trials and tribulations in life in order to become our truth, we need to be really proud of our true self, and what we've achieved.

Having lived our lives to the full, we would have all taken on board the emotional insecurities that will affects us, but not really knowing that we had but even so they play an important part within our characters. Sometimes we are left feeling bewilderment of our own doing, the instinctive reaction to the hurts, betrayals and so on. At times we walk around in a mental fog, in protective armour, our lower self-responding to that of a victim. We can a lot about a person and to what's happened to them by their body language, the physical body then portraits the imbalances within. So by being able to view the physical body can tell you a lot about what is in fact going on within.

For example if your physical body leans to the left you have imbalances within the feminine side of your body, which could also include the organs etc. to the left side of the body. If your body leans to the right, it's about the masculine side of your body, also to include the organs to the right side of the body. In fact the imbalances are present in our gestures, the way we walk, stand, even to how we fold our arms in a protective manner. Our hands can also tell us a lot about how we are feeling, the fingers showing us the minor details to our imbalance or disharmony. Even to what we say, or to what we do not say, also tells us a lot about what is going on within and around us. For the most important attribute we have is the physical body, because every unique characteristic will show us the reasons and the understandings, to our lessons that we need to learn.

Within in the physical body is all that we need to maintain a healthy life, we have all the natural resources and abilities to achieve our full potential, in what we truly desire. When we understand the powerful concatenations of our actions and interactions on all levels of existence, and of the characters that we've become over many incarnate lives, we will all deal with things some of unpleasant life experiences will cause us to close down or to turn in on ourselves, we all need contact and support from our loved ones, but at times not letting them in. We must remember that we are all a big part of the family of life, so we must help one another to overcome the difficult times.

When we recognise where we are denying the self, will enable us to take the first step to helping ourselves, as we all need to be touched and held, and to be loved, we need support but most importantly we need to be encouraged when we feeling down. Without the love and support, we would lead a very lonely existence, and through deep loneliness we would not able to function properly. We all need our families, as we're not meant to be alone, especially in our times of need, so we must not be afraid to seek the help that we need when life becomes too much.

We need to recognise our self-worth, but we also need to appreciate the worth of others too, when we help others we are in fact helping ourselves. When others help us they are helping themselves too, it's realising that we're all interconnected. We need to be aware of all things; we need to be aware that the objective of an earthly life as we know it, is so we can achieve peace within ourselves, then to allow the peace to radiate from within, outwards eventually helping other achieves their peace.

So the truth is hidden from us, so remember, the secret is to travel the universe to find it, the fact is, only after living

144

our lives to the full will we find the truth hidden deep within our hearts and souls, so it's alright if it takes us a lifetime, and beyond to find it. It's only by living our life, and being aware of the imbalances, and disharmony within that we realise that something is missing. Then we'll be in a position, to reconnect to the essence of our personal truth. When we find it we'll be so overwhelmed, that we're in awe that we've found it, it's the greatest gift that we can give to us. It's only then that we realise the importance of putting our-self first this is not a selfish act, and it's everybody's responsibility to undertake his or her own inner journey. Then we'll know sheer joy that we've found it, and we're able at last to become our truth and infinite power.

This is our life, and it's no rehearsal, so make the most of it, we are the most important person in our lives, so take notice to witness your own life first, because by allowing others to take precedence, the only person being deceived is our-self. We have to help our-self in reclaiming our lives back, and to take full control of having the star role within our own life. This is then the first big lesson that we do indeed learn, and it's the only lesson that successfully takes us home, to reside within the heart because home is where the heart is.

So for all of us, life is what we make it, so how would our lives be when we had successfully completed the souls quest? We would be an enlightened soul, where we'd be in a privileged position, to take enlightenment all the way, if we so desired and if that's what was intended for us. Our physical bodies vibrate at a level of conscious awareness, so depending on the level of awareness that we in fact came into this physical life with, will denote the level of consciousness which we vibrate at in order to overcome our lessons, of this lifetime.

The way that it works is, that with every lifetime we've had, and with the different situations or circumstances we've experienced and right down to the lessons that we've learned, will form a scale of logarithmic consciousness, a scale that records our level of truth to date. On a scale of one to ten, one is the lowest level of consciousness, and ten being the highest level of consciousness and that of enlightenment. So with every lifetime that we have, our level of consciousness goes up with the lessons learned, and does the perception of our truth of those learning's. We will all have had lifetimes, where we didn't have to learn the lessons, so our consciousness stayed the same, maybe because others had lessons to learn from us, like karmic debt or even the fact that we'd earned this lifetime being highly evolved. But whatever the case, we came into this life on a level of conscious awareness, with the potential to raise our vibrations when we'd fully understood the significance to our existence. So when we had successfully accomplished level ten, we could then go onto accomplish enlightenment.

In enlightenment there are levels of consciousness to attain, but in whichever life we're in, we'll achieve the ultimate state of awareness, because with every level that we've achieved, will be the level we've aspired too. As with all illusions in life, we can also create a spiritual state of illusion, but this again, is about our level of truth, because, we cannot prove that the mystical gifts of the unknown are real along with the spiritual phenomena. We under-estimate our uniqueness of our true selves, and to the knowledge and wisdom that we've already attained, but also, to the inner knowing of the secrets that are deep within us, and we'd attained a very long time ago.

Enlightenment is a state that we'll achieve naturally, it cannot be forced or brought, this state of awareness is like our truth and it has to be reconnected with. So like all the wonders of the world, they are not just for the selected few, they are for everyone to attain, we just need to let go of all the controls, free fall into nothingness and their deep within ourselves is the gifts of eternal bliss. We all need to feel content, joyful, and blissfully happy within ourselves and this happens once our state of conscious awareness as been achieved. Who's to say that we've not already achieved this ultimate state, in order for

146

us to be living abundantly within our chosen lifestyle, no that is, but us? So what is right for us, is not necessarily right for someone else, everyone will know deep within himself or herself, they're own personal levels of truth. The truth of the matter is, as long as we're our truth in every-way, and that we're living the life the way that we're meant too then deep within us we'd be at peace, feeling happy and content in all you do, and our physical body being healthy on every level of our being.

Throughout our lives we will all expose ourselves to the different vibrations from people, places and situations. Even the books we read, the holistic cultures and techniques that we embrace, music, art, in fact, in all that we do, say, think and feel will have a level of consciousness. So as long as we do the things that are for our highest good then we'll raise our level of consciousness. But the down side is that if we expose ourselves to the things that are not to our highest good, they will affect us in negative ways and only feed our lower conscious self. That's what life is all about, taking the highs with the lows, and to know the difference, allowing our perception to influence what we do, and then how we act upon our interpretation of that information will make all the difference to our lives. So remember we do not have to put up with anything that we're not happy with, as long as we can honestly say that we've given it our best efforts, and did everything within our power to achieve a positive outcome for all.

In understanding and overcoming the different situations, we can then move onto the next chapter of our lives. When all is said and done, the decisions that we do make are the ones that we're supposed to make at that particular time. The truth is we do have the power to make the choices, changing our lives for the better in order to become our true selves. But in accepting all that we do and as long as we live in the Now! When the time becomes right we can change our minds and move onto other things we can, as long as we have fun in all that we do.

147

We must all maintain an outer show of confidence, portraying the self-image of success, and encouraging us to be honourable, whilst fulfilling our obligation to the promises we made. These places us in good stead for our future growth and in all that we do, thus maintaining an inner equilibrium. We then play the star role in the production of our lives, and remember no one said we should be unhappy; it's just our perception of how we deal with the lessons that creates the unhappiness. So if there is a part of your life that you're not happy with, do something about it while you've the chance too, the mirror images are there to help us all overcome, and life's purpose and embrace the good times.

When the times right what we need will present its self to us, in order for us all to understand the bigger picture to life, with us rejoicing in the opportunities that life as given us; in order to accomplish our dreams, and manifesting all that we desire, but only if we completely live in our truth. When the time becomes right, we'll evolve to the next level of conscious awareness, evolving until we've successfully activated the bridge of the lower consciousness, to the higher consciousness, allowing us to reach the enlightened state of awareness that gives us access to the only real wealth that we can successfully take with us through life, and then onto the next stage of the souls journey or quest.

The journey from the material world, to the spiritual evolution of the continuance of the soul's journey, is life changing. Our material world anchors us to the lower consciousness, with us holding onto the material for the wrong reasons, which slows the process of attaining the higher conscious state. We at times hold onto our material wealth for support, comfort, and in misguided growth of the soul's purpose, because it chains us to the perception that it will make us happy.

The importance of unity in all things brings world peace and harmony within, because this is what life teaches us, to live together as one big family, and to understand the different

148

concepts of the lessons that we've all agreed to learn. In other lifetimes we would have experienced all aspects of life in different circumstances and situations, with our beliefs being different to this lifetime. These learning's are just other aspects of the truth, with life's experiences influencing us all, but we need to experience them in order to see a much bigger picture of what life and our existence, is all about.

The truth is, we are all right in the choices that we do in fact make, because we are being influenced by a powerful force, and the vibrational power of the real us, and all that we've ever achieved. When it comes down to the real truth, it's just one God, one life force energy; everything else is the illusions of life. It's important that we do learn these valuable lessons, while we still have a chance of enjoying life to the full, with us all reaching our limitless potentials. We are recycled souls, experiencing all walks of life with the different situations and circumstances influencing us. With time and patience, we will endeavour to succeed to the understanding that we're all equal, because it's not just about this lifetime, but that of other lifetimes too. Where we'll have played all of the different roles, within society, and the family of life, teaching us to become none judgmental, for we'll have experienced the different emotional traits, their actions and consequences.

Each and every-one of us, will have had it all, and will have lost it all, the secret to life is not to feel threatened by what we think is missing within our lives. If we only focus on what we feel we do not have or on what we think we want or need, we actually miss the opportunity to rejoice in what we do in fact have, a life! We miss so much in life because we give our power away to chasing rainbows; we give our power away when we only focus on the negative issues of the situations that we find ourselves in, instead of looking for the positive ones, which comes from the learning's of our lessons. All we need to do, is to realise how lucky we are, taking stock of all the things that we do have, and to what we've already achieved.

The deeper fundamental learning's are that we will have achieved the knowledge and wisdom that comes from living our lives to the full, to know what we can change, and to have the wisdom to know what we can't change, and to be accepting of that. To live our lives with all aspects of human nature, and to ensure that we've allow ourselves the opportunity to accept the lessons given, gracefully, and to understand that even while we're making hard work of life, the experiences to know the difference, is all we need.

The most important is the learning's, because the vibrations of which, we take with us, from lifetime to lifetime, to the higher vibrational planes of all existences. So in this lifetime we can access those important learning's in order to activate the vibrations from long ago, of the infinite knowledge and wisdom. This life is about fine-tuning the worn out soul, to liberate us into the twenty first century of the evolutionary journey of enlightenment, and continuance of our soul.

We are now living in The Golden Age of Aquarius. Our pre-destiny awaits us, with us enjoying the simple pleasures of life, and living our lives to the full, with us all following our hearts desires, dreams and goals.

CONCLUSION

What we make of our lives is up to us, it's is our ability to understand what we want from life and to take it. Life really does work out the way it's supposed too. All that is required from us is the courage and determination to succeed, and the commitment to be living our lives to the full, readjusting to the different vibrations and levels of our existence, and our conscious awareness and truth. To be accepting of all life's experiences, and rejoice in the many opportunities that is given to us in so many ways, making our lives so rich and rewarding. To go with the flow of life because to go against the flow, creates hardship and sorrow. The higher consciousness knows the truth to our lifetime, so to be still and go within, reconnect us to our true-self.

It is important to give ourselves the opportunity to hear the inner voice that whispers words of comfort or reassurance in our times of need, and the voice that would allow a sense of calm to prevail in the eye of the storm. We are so busy within our lives that we do not give ourselves the opportunity to listen to the higher consciousness, of the inner self, often depriving ourselves of the information that would allow us to conduct ourselves in an unattached manner that would give us the solutions to deal with the crisis in hand, without the need to hold on to the anguish, and heartache that creates the unrest of the soul.

To be our true selves, is to be honest with what we want from life, and to be truthful in our desires. We need to be prepared to take responsibility to the outcome to any endeavour, and to accept that whatever happens was meant to happen. To understand the lessons in life, and to move on to the next challenge by not feeling threatened in any way. Beating ourselves up, only creates the disharmony that eventually creates the unhappiness that we then hold ourselves too. Unhappiness is just an unjustified state of

151

unrecognised abilities and potential, thinking that we have to act in a particular way to the different situations or circumstances that we may find ourselves in.

To justify our feelings is to give our power away, by doubting the self. We are all unique individuals, different in every possible way, right down to how we perceive the different situations within our lives. We must ensure that when we question or feel unsure about what's going on in our lives that we stop, and ask ourselves what it is that's really going on. For our insecurities is just part and parcel of what is really wrong within our lives, so what is wrong? Our perception of our thoughts, feelings and actions, beating ourselves up because we think we've got it wrong, not recognising that we are in fact creating disharmony from being negative, maybe focusing on what we've no control over, instead of focusing on what we do have control of. Our positive actions and interactions of our thoughts, and feelings, and living in the now for the right reasons, and accepting all experiences as positive learning's of our lessons. Do not buy into the thought process that we're hard done too, and that it has only happened to us. Negative things happened to all of us at some time or other or maybe in another lifetime, long ago.

So just remember to have faith in yourself, skills and abilities, and to recognise your own worth and limitless potential. Do not feel threatened by the decisions of others, and be accepting of all things, good or bad. Only look for the positives in all situations, and do not give your power away, worrying about the things you have no control over. Stay powerful and connected to your dreams and desires, keeping a strong focus on what you want to achieve. Treat others as you would have them treat you, and do not hold onto anything that's not about your highest good. When we feel insecure, we need to understand why, and try to live by the Laws of the Universe, allowing yourself to be the real you, and to becoming your truth. Allow everyone to excel at their own pace and time, and to be tolerant and kind to those less fortunate than us. To know that everyone is right in what they do, and living by their own levels of truth. Trust that all will be revealed in divine timing, and to honour and respect all of life. To love yourself with all of your imperfections, and to practice unconditional love for all, with you witnessing your life first, before witnessing others. We must rejoice in all opportunities, and be aware of the synchronization of events that if acted upon could change our lives forever. Good Luck!

My next book is called Parallel Lives, A book about the intriguing aspects of how our lives are influenced by the negative traits of our learning's from previous lifetimes, gaining the understanding of the different aspects of which we really are, and the characteristics that form our personalities. With us eventually understanding the significance of how we can turn our lives around, using the positive attributes of all lifetimes, bringing the wonderful gifts, skills and abilities into this lifetime, living our lives as was intended by our creator. A lifetime enriched, our full potential acknowledged and realised, living life abundantly with the manifestation of all your dreams and desires, a powerful life, a life of eternal bliss, giving you back the power of the universal energies that sustains a healthy, happy and rewarding life, a life really worth living.

If you would like to get in touch with me to ask questions or even to voice your own theories or experiences.

My email address veronicalavender@btinternet.com

My websites:

www.veronicalavendersholisticevents.co.uk

www.veronicalavender.com

Good Luck and every success for your future.

Made in the USA
Columbia, SC
20 May 2017